To Dr. Stephen Livesay—

May God bless you and your ministry in all ways.

Henry Morris
Prov. 14:12

FULL PARDON

The Harry L. Greene Story

As told to Robert C. Larson

Good News Publishing
2230 E. Parham Rd.
Richmond, VA 23228

FULL PARDON

All Scripture quotations are taken from the King James
Version.

Good News Publishing
2230 E. Parham Rd.
Richmond, VA 23228

Editor: Rachel Derowitsch
Cover and interior design: Robert Greuter & Associates

ISBN 0-8474-5558-0

Printed in the USA

Dedication

To my wife, Barbara, my son, Matthew, and my daughter,
Sara, who, aside from my salvation, are God's greatest gifts
to me. Your love, encouragement, support and prayers
have been the foundation for all I have accomplished as
President of Good News Jail & Prison Ministry.

Acknowledgments

Dr. William L. Simmer — My spiritual father, mentor, and friend who never gave up on me. I owe what I am today to this man of God.

Mrs. Helen Simmer — Bill's wife and co-founder of the Good News Ministry. She was truly the example of the godly woman written about in Proverbs 31. She became a second mother to me.

Rev. Lawrence R. Katz — My best friend who was my pastor for ten years and is a long time member of the Good News Board of Directors. He has been used of God in my life in many ways.

Robert W. Thompson — Chairman of the Board of Directors of Good News. His leadership and friendship have been a special blessing and I have learned much from him.

John M. Gregory — Good News Board of Directors member who has been mightily used of God in our ministry and many others as well. His heart for souls and how he lives out Matthew 25:33-45, are a testimony and example to all who serve the Lord with him.

Philip E. Van Gorp, Vice President and Chief Operating Officer of Good News — his loyalty, friendship, commitment to God and Good News, along with his remarkable administrative skills, have ministered to me and encouraged me in more ways than I could ever relate.

Robert C. Larson — Author of *Full Pardon,* and over 60 other books. His love for the Lord, tremendous writing abilities, commitment to excellence, integrity, and patience have been an inspiration to me as we began, worked through, and completed *Full Pardon.*

Foreword

Full *Pardon* is more than the Harry L. Greene story. It is that, but it's much more. It's the story of how God pursues us as the Hound of Heaven and will not let us go. It's the story of a godly grandmother who would not quit praying for her grandson. It's the story of two men whose lives will be intertwined forever. It's the story of the difference one faithful servant of God can make when he is always there for you.

From his boyhood days in the Appalachian foothills to becoming an Army deserter and finally a prisoner in the Virginia State Penitentiary, Harry Greene freely admits that his early life was all about Harry Greene. He was full of himself, his goals and ambitions, his pursuit of the good life. That's the way he lived his life, and likely would have continued to live his life had he not met another man who was equally filled with Harry Greene. That man was Chaplain William Simmer.

I have known Bill Simmer for more than two decades and he is all that Harry says he is in *Full Pardon*. He is ex-Air Force, quick stepping, straight back, tough as nails and tender as the Savior when it comes to the hearts of men. This book is as much about the relationship between Bill Simmer and Harry Greene as it is about Harry Greene's unlawful past or prison life.

Throughout the book you will sense the author's deep respect and love for the chaplain God used to bring him to Himself. This is a book about influence, about mentoring, about persistence, about never giving up. It's about two men who are real life, modern-day counterparts of Moses and Joshua. It's not a story in praise of men, for as you read you will find yourself drawn to God and His "love that will not let me go."

God is using Harry Greene and Good News Jail & Prison Ministry chaplains to reach into the hearts of men and women throughout the USA and around the world. Whenever I see the hand of God blessing a ministry I always want to look into the lives of those who guide that ministry. Could God's blessing be tied to their integrity, to their pliability in the Potter's hand, to their compassion for the lost? That's usually the case and when you read *Full Pardon* and gain insight into the lives of those God has used to give birth and future vision to this ministry, you know that's the case as well with Good News Jail & Prison Ministry.

You will be inspired by this story, but don't stop there. You will be informed about life in prison, but don't stop there. Read with an open heart and ask God, "What role do You have for me in reaching into the hearts of those living behind bars?" Only then can we truly experience the impact of what it means to have a *Full Pardon*.

> Dr. Woodrow Kroll
> President and Senior Bible Teacher
> Back to the Bible
> Lincoln, Nebraska

Contents

Chapter 1

Into the Pit

The number of inmates in state and federal prisons has increased more than fivefold, from less than 200,000 in 1970 to more than 1,210,000 today. An additional 592,000 are held in local jails.

Bureau of Justice statistics

I t was 7:30 P.M. on June 10, 1964, when a subdued, John Wayne-handsome—and handcuffed—six-foot, three-inch Harry Greene arrived under armed guard at the Arlington County (Virginia) Jail to begin paying his debt to society. Within minutes, the big, brash twenty-year-old had gone from flying high with a steady diet of wine, women, and song to the more sobering fare of questionably safe water, half-crazed fellow inmates, and the incessant blare of a raspy loudspeaker careening off the "tank's" shiny, bare walls—all from which there would be no escape for a very long time. Harry had prided himself on an uncanny ability to generate new and exciting experiences: new women, new scams, new cars, new and luxurious hotels, and new ways to con banks into thinking the money he was withdrawing was actually his own. It seldom was. Landing in jail was a new experience, too. It wasn't what Harry had imagined would be his next new experience. There were probably as many warrants out for his arrest as there were bad guys in the booking area where he was logged in, photographed, and fingerprinted. The warrants did not go unnoticed.

"So who are you, anyway? Harry Adams, Richard Wayne Geary, Richard Wayne Adams, or Harry Greene?" asked the officer, throwing out the names of some of the aliases Harry had used during his crime spree. Harry admitted that he was

Harry. Harry L. Greene. They took his belt, shoelaces, and jewelry as they readied him for the tank. "Do you want to call a lawyer?" asked the booking officer. Harry had about $2,500 cash in his pocket—enough to buy the legal prowess of a smart-enough mouthpiece to get him out of this stinking place, he figured. "I don't know any lawyers," Harry said coolly. "Maybe you could recommend one." In prison or out, money talks, and the fat wad of hard currency shouted loudly enough to get Harry a good lawyer—but not good enough or soon enough to prohibit the young prisoner from spending the first night of his loss of freedom in the tank—or the "receiving cell," as it is more politely called.

The tank Harry found himself in was clean, according to jail standards, but it still stunk to high heaven.

The tank has its own culture. Its own environment. Its own unforgettable smell. It's the first place everyone who's arrested goes before they get their day in court, or are bound over to the grand jury and set for trial. The tank Harry found himself in was clean, according to jail standards, but it still stunk to high heaven. *Why don't they clean up this mess? Don't our taxes provide at least for a cleaning crew?* he thought. The drunks that night were puking all over themselves and on each other. Some who had been high on whatever were starting to crash like loose pieces of a glacier smashing wildly into the sea. There was no air-conditioning; just rickety old fans that would barely budge the stench of the warm, suffocating air. These folks were not exactly what you'd call the pillars of society.

The first thing that gets the attention of prisoners when

they land in the tank is the sound of the *door*—that heavy metal object, that goes into that heavy frame, that lodges itself into that inhospitable, massive concrete housing. It's a door that reverberates and shakes the wall so violently when it slams shut that everyone who hears and feels it knows one thing for certain: *I'm in jail, locked up, and I'm not going to be visiting any friends, lovers, or fellow con artists anytime soon.* Those were also the reflections of young Harry Greene as he paced the night away, anxiously surveying the floor, walls, and ceiling of the large, dorm-like tank on that first disorienting night of captivity, where he now had a ringside seat to some of the best examples of human depravity—a low-achieving group of which he had suddenly become an honorary member.

Today's jails and prisons are more modern and humane than what Harry experienced; his tank had not yet caught up to what would one day be a movement toward prison reform, although the Arlington County Jail was probably more innovative and forward thinking than most jails at the time, largely because of the influence of Sheriff J. Elwood Clements.

"I didn't sleep a wink that first night," Harry remembers. "I just walked back and forth, my emotions going wild. Mostly, I was just plain angry. I couldn't believe I'd actually been busted for my crimes and was now in this filthy place with filthy people I would never spend two minutes with on the outside."

Jail had the singular power to organize Harry's thoughts—fast—and the young prisoner, who'd not yet reached his twenty-first birthday, began to think about the night before, when he was luxuriating in a five-star hotel, driving a rented Cadillac, enjoying the sexual services of all the girls he could muster, plying them with non-stop booze, and drinking the night away. There was still more than $5,000 worth of designer suits hanging in his hotel closet. Now this.

From champagne to sewage within twenty-four hours. This was not supposed to happen—especially not to the invulnerable, worldly-wise Harry Greene. It was a sudden spiral downward from the Ritz to the pits. From the splendor of a glitzy hotel suite to the tank, where the toilet and drinking machine were one and the same—something Harry will never forget.

"This was also a drunk tank, so guys were throwing up all over this unique water fountain/urinal device. Welcome to Arlington County Jail."

"The toilets were fixed so that you could run drinking water through them," Harry recalls. "You just put your finger in a hole so the water would gush up, and you could drink it. You could also pull your finger out and wash your hands. The wonders of engineering. Oh, yes, it was also used as a urinal. This was also a drunk tank, so guys were throwing up all over this unique water fountain/urinal device. Welcome to Arlington County Jail."

As Harry continued to walk the floor of the tank that night, one thought kept running through his mind: *How am I going to get out of this pit?* He had the cash to make bond, which meant he'd pay the money, take off, assume yet another false identity, and never be heard from again. But with so many warrants hanging around his neck, he knew it wasn't going to happen.

He was right. The next morning, a Friday, a rumpled Harry Greene was informed that a grand jury had filed charges of forgery and grand larceny against him. After a hasty court appearance, Harry was escorted back to jail—but this time away from the tank to a cell block where the immature, cocky, soon-as-hit-you-as-look-at-you young punk discovered his new home. Home? You've got to be kidding! As the corrections offi-cer (or CO) led Harry down the hall to Cell Block C, the sights and sounds of incarceration hit him like a batch of bad prison food: there was shouting and cursing, with half-naked prison-ers spitting and urinating, screaming at hapless COs and at their fellow inmates who were leaning against the bars as they gazed vacantly into space. Suddenly it dawned on the young man where he was and what he had done to get here. And an even bigger issue now weighed on his mind: *How long before he'd be released?*

Harry went into the slammer on a warm summer night in 1964, when the modernization and privatization of our penal institutions did not enjoy the priority they receive today. But modern or ancient, cruel or compassionate, jail is jail and prison is prison. Then and now. As Harry stepped into his cell, he asked himself: *What do these clowns behind bars do all day? How do they adjust? With the endless hours, days, and years on their hands, what do they think about—or do they think at all?* Harry hasn't forgotten what he discovered so many years ago.

"It always comes down to the individual at some point determining I am going to break the law and ignore the consequences."

"There I was, blaming everyone and everything in the world except myself for my problems. That's what most inmates do. It's tough to get prisoners to admit they are responsible for where they are in their lives. They want to lay that blame on somebody else—where they grew up, the father they never knew, the abuse they suffered as a child. No doubt these may be contributing factors to their sad state of affairs, but it always comes down to the individual at some point determining *I am going to break the law and ignore the consequences.* I know, because that was the way I was thinking as I sat there in my world, which had now shrunk to the humble dimensions of the habitat of a caged animal."

Harry's new associates were a varied lot: ten inmates in Cell Block C from ages eighteen to sixty-five, with crimes ranging from traffic offenses to murder. There was no segregation of youthful offenders, first-time offenders, or hard felons. A prisoner was simply thrown into a block, and so it was with young Harry. Suddenly, without the freedoms he'd for so long taken for granted, he was now told when to get up, when to go to bed, when to exercise, when to eat, what to eat, when to shower, when to shave, and what wardrobe to wear—which in his case was an old pair of ill-fitting khaki jail clothes. This big boy was accustomed to better. How was he going to manage?

Harry quickly learned that one of the most frightening things about doing time behind bars is the speed with which prisoners adapt to the conditions of their incarceration. "In a matter of hours, my world became thirty feet long and twenty feet wide, with five cells in it. Whatever I might have been doing during the day, I dutifully returned to my cage each night, where they locked me up again as if I were an animal. I now lived in a zoo for people—a zoo I entered because of some terrible choices I had made in my life. But I had made those choices, and I was now suffering the inevitable consequences. I had no freedom, no friends, no family, and no future. I felt everyone in my cell block was staring at me, wondering who I was, how bad I was, and what I'd done to land in this wretched place. I had always enjoyed being the center of attention in my hard-living, scamming, roller-coaster life on the outside. Now, for the first time in my life, I didn't much appreciate being in the limelight.

There's a hierarchy in every cell block or prison: one person is always in charge, at least as far as the prisoners are concerned. Who these leaders are quickly becomes apparent. That's why inmates learn to be careful about what they say and to whom they say it. The whole atmosphere of a cell block is charged with fear and hesitancy. You hesitate to move around; you hesitate to talk to people; you hesitate to say too much or too little; you hesitate to make the wrong friends. You're always watching your back. In jail, a prisoner learns to rely on no one until he's developed some degree of trust. Even then, no one dares to get too close. Things change. Even cell block leadership changes. Prisoners have to be careful, because they never know what might happen.

Compared with prisons, jails are much more closely watched. COs are always walking up and down the catwalks and prisoners are always in plain sight. There are floor-to-ceiling bars, and then there's the cell block. Prisoners live in a goldfish bowl morning, noon, and night. However, no smart prisoner takes his safety and security for granted. Never. Harry learned those rules quickly; it made no difference if his new associates where young, old, bright, or dull. He learned quickly to be alert—and to watch his rather sizeable back—at all times.

Harry's first cellmate was a sixty-seven-year-old alcoholic, a man with that watery-eyed, emaciated, pink appearance who had been locked up for drunk driving.

Harry's first cellmate was a sixty-seven-year-old alcoholic, a man with that watery-eyed, emaciated, pink appearance who had been locked up for drunk driving. During the two days he and Harry were together, they didn't say more than three words to each other.

The next guy to share Harry's cell was a fellow named Lynn, who was second in command of the American Nazi Party under George Lincoln Rockwell, the party's founder. He was a giant of a man, with a shaved head and Nazi tattoos all over his body. He was mean as a snake and probably the most bigoted guy Harry had ever met—especially when it came to spitting out incessant vitriol against blacks and Jews and other minority groups. Lynn had been arrested at a hate rally that had quickly turned into a riot. In the center of the ongoing melee was big Lynn, beating up on those who did not espouse his views. The authorities rightly figured the man needed some time to cool off. Harry remembers, "I'm pretty sure Lynn was also guilty of a few other things the authorities knew nothing about. Over time we began to talk, and eventually we became pretty good friends. It's amazing the kinds of relation-ships you develop in prison—with people you wouldn't give the time of day to on the outside."

It is in this atmosphere of hate, anger, and denial that Christian chaplains find their mission. It is not an easy assignment.

What jail is really all about is *passing time*. Time crawls and stalls. The numbers on the calendar seem to be set in stone. Prisoners are convinced there are more than twenty-four hours in a day, at least ten days in a week, and more than 365 days in a year. Try 3,650! So they play cards, talk, argue, connive, scam, and brag about their women, how much they could drink, and how sexually potent they were in the *good old days*. Studs all—or so these male prisoners would have you believe. Such bravado is the core of jail dialog—frivolous, meaningless chatter—something to pass the long, tedious hours. It is in this atmosphere of hate, anger, and denial that

18

Christian chaplains find their mission. It is not an easy assignment. But as Christian chaplains keep coming back to the cell
blocks day after day, making friends of the prisoners, talking
about sports or whatever else is of interest to the men, they
begin to share the Good News of Jesus Christ. This is when the
tone of the conversations slowly begins to change; and when
the Person of Jesus Christ finally enters a prisoner's heart of
stone, He sets him free and changes his life for eternity.

This has been the calling of Good News Jail & Prison
Ministry for more than forty years—a mission of committed
Christian chaplains who have hung in there with some of our
toughest prisoners, loving, teaching, and simply *being there*
when inmates have needed them most. It is our prayer that in
the following pages you will see more clearly than ever the
need for chaplains in our jails and prisons, both at home and
abroad, who will continue to share this Good News with the
thousands of men and women who right now are behind
bars. This is the mission of Good News Jail & Prison
Ministry—and the only reason we are telling you the Harry
Greene story.

"I was a gang leader, always looking to prove something or build a reputation as the baddest guy there was. I drank a lot, but later went to drugs, which led to my incarceration. I first met the Good News chaplain during a church service, and when I talked to him, he was helpful. As a result of this ministry, I have trusted Christ and have begun to make changes in my life.

"What turned me from crime was trusting Christ as my Savior while I was in jail. During Bible class, Ephesians 4:22–24 became meaningful: 'Put off . . . the old man, which is corrupt according to the deceitful lusts; and be renewed in the spirit of your mind; and . . . put on the new man, which after God is created in righteousness and true holiness.'

"My life has changed dramatically! I knew the Lord could do it. Not only has He done it, but He gives me strength to continue steadfast in His ways. I don't even have the desire to do anything contrary to His Word."

— A changed life

Chapter 2

Where the Lights Never Go Out

Remember them that are in bonds, as bound with them.

Hebrews 13:3

T hough Harry quickly became a leader among his fellow inmates—visibly demonstrating his "boss" qualities from his first few days in jail—there was one little thing that just about drove him crazy: *the lights in his cell block were never turned off.* Never. When it was time to bunk down, there was no handy bedside switch to kill the lights overhead. When sleep became difficult and Harry would wake up in the middle of the night, the lights surrounding him would still be burning brightly. No matter how hard he would squash the flimsy pillow over his head, or whether he buried himself under a thin, gray blanket, or closed his eyes so tightly that he saw stars, the lights kept burning . . . and burning . . . and burning. The COs had to be able to see the prisoners at all times, and the twenty-four hours of light in the cell block made that possible. Harry remembers, "It probably took me a week to ten days to get used to the idea that there would always be light in Cell Block C, and that I would simply have to learn to sleep with its glare. I hated it. It was a nuisance and an inconvenience. But then, jail is designed to be an inconvenience."

When Harry was released years later, he was completely unaccustomed to the dark. That's why the first few nights of freedom terrified him. "Here I was, a big ex-con, supposedly toughened by my years of incarceration, but afraid of the darkness, as if I were a small child," he recalls. "As soon as it would get dark in my new surroundings, I would reach over and turn on a lamp. I remember how I'd almost panic until I could find the switch and turn on enough light to flood my room. I think I slept with the lights on for at least two weeks until I got used to the dark.

"Prison gets you accustomed to lots of things that surprise you: you either adapt or you snap; you get with the program, or you go nuts. I decided early on that rather than go crazy, it made more sense to bury my head in a pillow and accept the inevitable. And that meant accept everything— even a cell block that was never dark."

> "Prison gets you accustomed to lots of things that surprise you. But you either adapt or you snap; you get with the program, or you go nuts."

You even learn to accept the food. For Harry, prison cuisine was far removed from the five-star dining to which he had become accustomed on the outside. How the food in jail was presented wasn't all that attractive, either. Harry reminisces, "There were floor-to-ceiling bars that ran the length of our cell block, and there was a small opening in the bars through which a tray of food could be passed. Underneath, a metal table about seven to eight feet long was welded to the bars, and then a bench with three supports was welded to that. That was where I ate my three daily meals—like a caged animal salivating for a bowl of whatever the daily fare might be. I had become comfortable with the room service in the hotels I had been defrauding over the past several months, and this new style of 'food presentation' was not exactly appealing. I hated the idea that the only time I was allowed to eat was when someone unceremoniously shoved my food through those cold, iron bars. It was demeaning. Dehumanizing. Still, one of the highlights of my day was getting something to eat—even if it was a poor substitute for a real meal. However, food also became a highly sought after 'currency' which we gambled for every single day."

Harry was big enough and tough enough to throw his weight around in the cell block, but he soon discovered that no inmate needed to have size on his side to participate—and do well—in the idle activity of gambling. Here, all prisoners played on a relatively level field. A bet was a bet, and all hell would break loose if a wager went unpaid. Any wager. On anything. *Food for gambling* became a prime commodity, which Harry worked for all it was worth. He would give the losers a little reminder of their debt: "'Okay, Joe, I won our little game of hearts *again,* and the bet was *your* lunch, remember, old buddy? So, when your lunch comes, just remember it's mine, okay? If you dispute that, then we have a little problem going between us, don't we?'"

Harry lost lunch and dinner, and he won lunch and dinner, because in jail and prison, you play for whatever you have that is of value, and nothing is more valuable than food—even lousy, cold, non-nutritious prison food. Your monetary system changes to what you have that might be worth something. In jail, the smallest item takes on monstrous proportions *when it's all you have.* Most jails and prisons have what they call a canteen fund, and if a prisoner has the money, the institution will give him a "ticket" and later come by with the "canteen wagon," from which inmates can buy candy or snacks, or whatever is available. It's a big moneymaker for jails; it's an even more important commodity for inmates because of its enormous economic and psychological value.

Harry remembers, "We played cards, chess, and checkers

for a piece of chocolate, cans of soda, shaving cream, meals, you name it. We bet on everything and anything, and the stakes were always something we perceived to be of value—items that, of course, would have been relatively worthless on the outside. I never once played a game in jail that wasn't *for* something. That was why a 'judge' would always stand behind one player to make sure the other guy wasn't cheating. But don't think for a moment that having a jailhouse referee made us honest citizens. There were always ways to beat the system."

And Harry could con the best of them. He remembers one creative way he and his pinochle partner used to cheat. "When you held the cards you'd been dealt," he says, "you pushed one card up slightly higher than the other. This would mean you were strong in hearts. If you pushed two cards up, that meant you were strong in spades. So, there were plenty of ways to get around the eyes of the judge. You just had to be smart about it."

It's probably safe to say that jail and prison don't so much make a prisoner what he is; more than likely, incarceration simply reveals who he already is.

Prison is all about adapting to what is happening at the moment. You learn to think—and cheat—fast. An inmate either figures out how to cope with his immediate situation, or he's out of luck. Simple as that. Those who couldn't or didn't cope well with the stress broke like toothpicks, a reaction that took many forms: anger, depression, paranoia, sadness, or convulsing in tears because they received an unexpected letter from their wife, or because their mother or daughter sent them something that touched them deeply. Many of these guys had never cried in their lives. Now they sobbed like babies. The jail experience suddenly provided the environment for pent-up feelings to take their late expression. It's probably safe to say that jail and prison don't so much make a prisoner what he is; more than likely, incarceration simply reveals who he already is. It's just a matter of time before the revelation becomes reality.

Jail and prison are great places to learn new things. Trouble is, they're usually the wrong things—the kind of information that will probably get you thrown back in behind bars as soon as you get out. Harry recalls, "In a matter of days, I learned how to crack a safe, where to get guns for rob-beries, how to boost a car, and where to find reliable informa-tion on good fences to help move stolen goods—fast. I was taking all of this information to heart, storing it away for future use. Then, during the second week I was in jail, it dawned on me: *If these guys sitting here in this cell with me are so smart, how come they're in here?* I began to realize that I was spending twenty-four hours a day with people who weren't all that good in their respective 'professions' after all. Further, I knew I'd never want to associate with a single one of them on the streets.

"I know today that I was no better than they were in God's eyes, but at the time, I saw them as a collective ragtag gang of losers, the scum of society. I felt I was better than all of them combined. Their values weren't as good as mine, and their former lifestyles couldn't hold a candle to the lav-ish lifestyle I once enjoyed on the outside. That's how I felt for a while—until it hit me that in jail that view of life amounts to *stinking thinking*, to use a phrase from the motivational speaker Zig Ziglar. It took me a while to recog-nize that when you're behind bars, you need to get along with everyone. Somehow. You just have to figure it out."

The Russian novelist Dostoyevsky writes in his classic

The Brothers Karamazov that "if God does not exist, every-thing is permissible." At the outset of his jail experience, this is precisely how Harry felt. Since there's no God, anything goes. Harry refused to believe in the existence of a Supreme Being; therefore, his worldview allowed for anything—good, bad, or indifferent. Yet, despite his hardness of heart, he still silently prayed that he would soon be released, hoping that his prayers would be answered. Would he receive a light jail sentence? A slap on the wrist? Be set free? Go to prison and do big time? Regardless of what his fate might be, to Harry, God would remain a cipher with the edges rubbed out: God was neither important nor relevant. Harry can still hear himself saying to the chaplain who was trying to reach out to him, "What I need is a good lawyer, man, not a dead Jew to get me out of this mess!" That pretty well sums up what Harry thought about the Almighty. With that attitude just about any-thing became permissible to Harry—as the Russian writer had insisted so long ago.

Harry can still hear himself saying to the chaplain who was trying to reach out to him, "What I need is a good lawyer, man, not a dead Jew to get me out of this mess!"

Harry will tell you, "You just can't get into a mind-set that says, 'I am going to like this guy and not that one.' If you think like this, *that* guy and you are going to come to blows sooner or later, and it's going to become very messy. You have to get along with everyone in your cell block. You don't have to like them, and they don't have to like you—and most of them will not like you. To prove my point, since my release I probably have not seen more than ten guys I did time with. I have no idea where all those guys are, and I went through a whole bunch of people while in jail and prison. I ate with them, slept in the same cell blocks with them, argued with them, swore with them, played cards by the hours with them, and had my meals with them. We did everything together. What other options did we have? However, we never bonded as friends. That's because none of us really liked each other. But we smart ones never admitted it. We just sucked it up, did our time—and, to pass the time, quietly beat as many of our fellow inmates at our nonstop card games as we possibly could."

One day a chaplain named William "Bill" Simmer poked his face into this angry, bad-attitude prison lifestyle Harry Greene was so proud of. Bill was now working in his third facility under Good News Mission, the ministry he founded in Fairfax, Virginia, in 1961. (The name was changed to Good News Jail & Prison Ministry in 1985.) Bill had also ministered in Alexandria, after which he came to Arlington. He came around far more than Harry would have liked. "The guy was *always* there—I mean, didn't he have better things to do with his life?" Harry would constantly ask himself. "We'd try to focus on our gambling, and there was Bill, sticking his nose through the bars of steel that caged us, talking, preaching, reading the Bible—all that religious nonsense. Some in our cell block saw him as genuine and friendly; I saw him as an intruder who kept interrupting my concentration as I dealt the cards. Many of my fellow inmates called him 'Rev' or 'Chap' or 'Chaplain' or 'Bill.' What I called him I don't want to put in print. I was totally unimpressed and could never understand what others saw in him."

Chaplain Bill Simmer had an Air Force background, and in the eyes of many of Harry's fellow inmates was a real man's man. He had seen the world, knew his way around, was mature, knowledgeable about many things, and freely discussed his views on life with any inmate who would listen. After resigning from the military, he became a successful building contractor in New England. One day, unexpectedly for Bill, someone introduced him to Jesus Christ. He learned that the Savior loved him for who he was and had a marvelous plan for his life. That encounter with God turned Bill's life around. Not only did God change his direction, but soon thereafter, Bill felt called to obtain a Bible school education. So he and his family moved to Arlington, Virginia, and he enrolled at Washington Bible College and Seminary in Washington, D.C. This same Bill Simmer was now the jail chaplain—and a person Harry avoided as if he had a bad rash. "But," says Harry, "when you're behind bars, and someone on the other side of those bars has something to say—and if he says it loudly enough—you don't have much choice but to listen, even if you despise the message."

As Bill would make the rounds, talking with the prisoners, he would often single out Harry and try to have a chat with him—something he actually managed to do on several occasions. "He would inform me that Christ loved me, died for me, rose again for me, blah, blah, blah," Harry recalls. "The last thing I wanted to hear was that kind of 'garbage.' In my opinion, there was nothing some unpopular Jew did 2,000 years ago that could affect my life today. That was my attitude, and I spoke it in no uncertain terms to this intrusive chaplain. I was hostile toward everything that sounded like God, Jesus Christ, or the church."

"But here's the important thing about this committed, dedicated chaplain: he was *always* there. It wasn't hit or miss. He showed up—every day. EVERY DAY! He became as much a fixture in our cell block as the COs, our meals, and our card games. But he didn't just stand there on the outside; he walked around, he talked with us, put his hand on our shoulder through the bars, loved us, cared about us. He even showed us Moody Science Films. Jails didn't have television or radios in those days, so to see a film—any kind of film, which reminded us of what we used to do outside—was a welcome sight. But why did the man have to keep yapping about God from morning till night?"

Chaplain Bill was always talking about the certainty of a relationship with Christ. That word *certainty* stuck in Harry's heart, because his whole life was one big *uncertainty*. He was cocky, brash, and hostile—but that didn't mean he was in control of his life. It was just another example of how good he was at denying reality. Actually, he hadn't the foggiest idea of what was going to happen next. Harry did know he was looking at the possibility of fifty-plus years in prison—something he admitted to himself that he deserved. Still, he was forever trying to manipulate his way out of doing more time, refusing to plead guilty. Big, tough Harry wasn't going to take this charge lying down. That was how it was for more than five months in Arlington County Jail—continuing to live like a caged animal, where the lights never went out—and where this pesky *Jesus guy* kept sticking his smiling face through the floor-to-ceiling iron bars.

Harry did know he was looking at the possibility of fifty-plus years in prison—something he admitted to himself that he deserved.

Chaplain Bill would come by on Sundays, hold church services, talk with the guys in the cell block, and take as much time as was needed to answer their questions—while Harry kept playing cards, keeping his distance, pretending not to hear a word. He didn't want to hear about God, Jesus, the Holy Spirit, the Bible, or any other religious hogwash. This straight-arm approach to what Bill was saying went on for several months. Then one day, something Bill said hit Harry like the proverbial ton of bricks. Harry had grown up in the church. He'd heard the Bible stories, gone to Sunday school, been bored to tears by endless sermons, and determined that religion would never be a factor in his adult life.

"I'd heard it all; I just didn't believe it," Harry says. "As a child, I had walked forward at a camp where my grandmother was representing Southern Baptist Bookstores. One night I made my way to the front of the altar after hearing an emotional message on salvation. I stepped out of my seat for one reason only: to please my grandmother, which, apparently, it did. But I didn't believe a word of what I'd just heard. I didn't believe in anything except the great Harry Greene. Still, I would continue to win prizes for memorizing Scripture verses, and had so many 'perfect attendance' pins from Sunday school that I walked lopsided. I was the greatest living example of someone *playing a role* you could ever find. The messages from those sincere pastors and evangelists went in one ear and out the other faster than you could say 'check forgery.'

"My family had always attended church, and growing up I would join them because I felt like I was made to go morning and night on Sunday, and to all those boring prayer meetings on Wednesday evenings. Now, the last thing I wanted to hear was more of this stuff while I was in jail—and part of a literally captive audience. Just the thought of being forced to hear about God and Jesus and heaven made me sick to my stomach. For months I was Cell Block C's poster boy that encompassed everything a chaplain is forced to endure—all of it bad."

Chaplain Bill enjoyed sports, history, politics—you name it—and he seemed to be conversant in just about any subject a prisoner wanted to talk about. Harry finally opened up to talking to Bill, as long as the conversation did not include religion. He didn't want to hear it, smell it, taste it, or have it infect his own thinking—which, incidentally, hadn't produced such impressive results to date, something that had not dawned on him at the time. Harry would one day be forced to admit that *if we are to discover life as God intended it for us, we must be ready to allow ourselves to be interrupted by this living God. If we assume our own schedules, our own agendas, and our own mind-sets are foremost in importance, we will never make it.* But that kind of thinking would come later. Much later.

Meanwhile, when it came to religion, Harry straight-armed Bill every step of the way. "I was hostile, angry and anti-God. Sports? Okay. God? Forget it! I remember when Bill would preach through the bars of our cell block and I'd roll my eyes, turn to my partner at the table, and say under my breath, 'Just deal 'em. Forget about that guy.'"

Forget about Bill? That was tough, because the next day, there he was again, standing outside the bars, preaching, sharing his faith, reading his Bible, talking about sports, and just being a friend to the inmates in Cell Block C. *What was it about a guy like this? What was in it for him? Why was he so concerned about prisoners?* As Harry looks back to those days in jail, he can still see Bill coming back day after day, regular as clockwork. It is a scene that Harry will take to his grave. A business guru once said that the *key to success in life, relationships, and business is just showing up.* Well, Bill apparently knew all about that philosophy, because he was always showing up. He was a man on a mission, telling inmates the truth about God, about the Person of Jesus Christ, and about themselves.

Harry began to accept that any failure in his life did not mean God had abandoned him, but simply that He had a better idea for Harry's future.

Full Pardon

One day Chaplain Bill's message of Christ's compassion and forgiveness finally made a small dent in the iron heart of big, bad Harry. To the young inmate, it was the equivalent of David's small stone penetrating Goliath's forehead. *Small stone, big effect.* What Harry did that day in the Arlington County Jail in the presence of Good News Chaplain Bill Simmer changed his life—and his view of the living God—forever. *Harry slowly began to accept that any failure in his life did not mean God had abandoned him, but simply that God had a better idea for Harry's future.*

Meanwhile, the electric lights in Harry's cellblock continued to burn day and night—something to which he had now become accustomed. However, for the first time in his life, the equally unquenchable light of God's love began to glow in all its brilliance in his softening heart. But before we share the story of his amazing conversion, it is important to know more about Harry's formation, to learn what made him tick, and, finally, to understand what led him to his life of crime that finally landed him in the Arlington County Jail—and worse places yet to come.

"I've been in prison thirteen years, altogether. I belong in prison. I was a danger to society and to myself. Everyone was terrified of me. I was a lost, confused soul, but several years ago I became a new soul. The person I am telling you about is dead. God used the Good News chaplain to help me understand my need to trust Christ, and I now acknowledge Him as my Savior.

"The chaplain also taught me to go beyond just studying the Bible and to begin using the tools it shows me in my spiritual battles.

"I'm now a trained soldier who understands his weapons and his mission. I will plant as many seeds as I can, and spread and teach about Jesus until I breathe my last breath."

— A grateful inmate

Chapter 3

But It All Started Out So Well

Despair is the absolute extreme of self-love.
It is reached when a man deliberately turns his
back on all help from anyone else in order to taste
the rotten luxury of knowing himself to be lost.
Thomas Merton

t was one of those bright, sweltering July afternoons in
Greeneville, not far from the Tennessee home of Andrew
Johnson, the American president who is probably best known
for suffering the indignity of an impeachment in 1868. The
Greenes' white clapboard house was a slice of Main Street
Americana—a suitable subject at any time of the year for the
likes of Norman Rockwell. The year was 1955, and country living was slow and easy. Contentment was in the air. Near the
Greene homestead were towns such as Bulls Gap, Mosheim, and
Chuckey. Not well known to the rest of the country, but for
local residents this was their universe. One road twenty-five
miles west of Greeneville, on the northern edge of the
Appalachian mountain range, proudly announced that "this
way" was the direction to the birthplace of Davy Crockett, one
of America's great, early nineteenth-century patriots who reflected his fellow citizens' thinking of the times when he said, "I am
at liberty to vote as my conscience and judgment dictates to be
right, without the yoke of any party on me. . . . Look at my arms,
you will find no party hand-cuff on them." On this summer day
in 1955, one could see near Crockett's birthplace an immense
barn with a large sign that expressed a more modern local sentiment: GET RIGHT WITH GOD.

Maggie Mae was in the kitchen, pressing thumb imprints
into a soft dough crust that was about to undergo the transfor-

mation into a luscious lemon meringue pie, while the pleasant smell of freshly baked bread from the stove found its way into every corner of the house. All the doors and windows of the house were thrown open wide, for the Tennessee heat and humidity held little respect for the wooden thresholds or fly screens. Only a small, black oscillating fan provided occasional relief, much like a soft, gentle breeze on an otherwise windless day. From a large, wooden, cathedral-style radio in the narrow hallway came the voices of *Burns and Allen*, punctuated by audience laughter—real laughter, not the canned laughs that giggle at today's mindless sitcoms. A rhythmic creaking would occasionally pierce the dialog of George and Gracie, a sound that echoed down the hall's oak wood floors and off the glass of the oval frames that proudly showcased the well-planted Greene family tree.

No need for store-bought toys. There were more than enough entertainment possibilities on the Greene homestead.

William (Bill) Greene was having a cigarette on the porch while watching eleven-year-old Harry run across the family's spacious yard, ducking under the large, old tree and trying to hide behind the weathered outhouse with his five-year-old brother, Dennis in hot pursuit. The two finally raced into the garage—their daily venue for exploring and playing imaginary games. As Harry ran over the dirt floor, shafts of light from shrunken planks threw backlighting on his dust trail. Long, hanging ropes and ancient wenches provided the perfect swinging environment for the two active country boys. No need for store-bought toys. There were more than enough entertainment possibilities on the Greene homestead.

Still immersed in their game, the two brothers almost didn't notice the approaching black roadster that was kicking up a plume of dust on the winding country road leading to the house. "Baba, Baba!" screamed Dennis. Harry heard the name of his beloved grandmother, bolted from the garage, and arrived in the front yard just as their black English shepherd, Duke, barked his noisy welcome. The large vehicle came so close to the house that columns of dust from the dirt road began falling on the freshly washed clothes drying on the line. Harry's mom heard the boys' gleeful screams and looked out the window. His dad looked up from his paper, noticed the boys running, and saw the approaching automobile. He yelled to Maggie Mae, 'Kitty's here.' Harry's mom wiped her hands on her gingham apron and smiled.

Kitty Sullivan, the boys' maternal grandmother, was a kind, loving soul, but her grandmotherly white hair could be deceptive. Kitty was a strong, independent woman. When her husband died in 1943, she resisted playing the role of a rocking chair widow, crocheting and knitting her days away, and resolved to remain active, if not aggressive, during the remaining years of her life. She would become a force to reckon with. "Now there's a godly woman if there ever was one," Harry would hear people say again and again. Although an ardent churchgoer, Kitty was never content to be a pew sitter. Not Kitty. She sat only when it was necessary; the rest of the time she was a woman in motion. Happy to be known as a good Christian and faithful witness, Kitty was always ready, eager, and willing to hear and heed God's call.

One day that call was especially loud—so deafening, in fact, that it prompted her to enroll in seminary—and that was in 1944, a time when women were hardly "liberated," it being only a scant three decades after women received the right to vote. That call from above was all Kitty needed to spur her on to a life as a religious leader, something she had desired for many years. Her decision to study theology was tolerated by a few; it was unbiblical to most. Kitty didn't really care. God had called her to service. Nothing else mattered.

Women did play a major role in the life of the church during the 1940s. After all, they were allowed to bake pies for church socials, arrange bouquets of flowers for their deacon husbands to take to hospital patients, use their singing talents in the church choir, play the organ, and teach Sunday school—and, of course, live as obedient wives to their husbands, always at their beck and call. But there was one hitch: women weren't allowed to be pastors, and since they couldn't be pastors by church law, there was no need to attend seminary, right? Well, for most people, but not for Harry's grandma. Kitty, true to herself, never did care much for church protocol, so she went to seminary anyway. It was all about *the call*. And she was not alone in her choice. There was actually one other woman in her class. A minority to say the least; a powerful example to other women to say the most. After graduation, Kitty continued to serve her God as a faithful missionary to the Eskimos in Alaska, about as far away from Tennessee as anyone could imagine.

> **Kitty, true to herself, never did care much for church protocol, so she went to seminary anyway. It was all about *the call.***

Harry and Dennis hadn't seen their grandmother in more than a year, another reason for all the excitement. In characteristic style, she emerged from the large roadster as Harry and Dennis ran straight into her arms, hugging her tightly. Mom Greene beamed from the front porch, knowing how much the boys had missed their *Baba*.

The next day being Sunday, Kitty joined the family as they set out for morning worship. *No one ever missed church in the Greene family.* In fact, Harry had already received his first gold cross, a lapel pin awarded to him for perfect Sunday school attendance. "Okay now, recite for me John 3:16," Kitty asked Harry in the car. Dutifully, Harry responded word for word . . . "For God so loved the world . . . ," reciting the words with military precision.

When they arrived for the morning service, the family could hear the musical prelude coming through the wide-open, white-panel double doors of the Mount Hebron Baptist Church. The old pump organ sounded slightly out of tune, but only the musically inclined noticed. At exactly 10:30, the iron bell in the steeple announced the moment of worship. During the service, the only audible noise, other than the high-volume preaching and singing, was the sound of donated, handheld funeral home fans that were used to help dissipate the heat. Harry remembers one fan had a picture of Jesus walking on water; another of Jesus talking to His disciples. Both cardboard pictures were stapled on wood sticks. Apparently the funeral directors of the region figured they'd landed on a workable marketing plan that provided a weekly reminder to parishioners of their transitory lives.

For Harry, the wooden pews were at a ninety-degree angle and were as uncomfortable as anything he'd ever sat on. But he sat anyway—like a good little soldier. His family had long been known for its military heritage, and Harry would often hear his father tell him about his most famous ancestor, Nathaniel Greene, a revolutionary war general for whom the town and Greene County had been named. The Greene clan had fought bravely in both world wars, many earning ribbons, medals, and other lapel-size tributes to their valor. As he now endured the oppressive heat and the flies that would occasionally buzz around his head, young Harry found his thoughts wandering off to the far-flung battlefields of the world, but not to the skirmish for people's souls—which would include his own. Harry could stomach the singing, but the sermon was what he feared most. The serious, unsmiling pastor would slowly trudge up the three steps to the platform and stand erect behind a wooden pulpit. To an eleven-year-old boy, the pastor appeared to be as large as a giant. "You are washed by the blood of the Lamb!" the pastor thundered, striking his fist on the pulpit with the force of a blacksmith striking an anvil. A few "amens" echoed in response. It scared Harry to death.

"You are washed by the blood of the Lamb!" the pastor thundered, striking his fist on the pulpit with the force of a blacksmith striking an anvil. It scared Harry to death.

It wasn't the content of the sermon as much as it was the intensity, energy, and the shouting that bothered him. As Harry sat with his back glued to the pew, he heard phrases, not sentences. He heard pitch and volume, but no message. He watched the pastor's gestures, but was oblivious to the large, white cross nailed to the front of the pulpit. Even at so young an age, Harry was learning to "become religious." He had figured out how to please his elders by reciting verses, attending Sunday school, giving all the right answers, and by sitting still and quiet during the service. *Look at Harry Greene. Isn't he a wonderful boy? God will certainly use him one day.* But God was neither real nor relevant. Harry remembers, "The end of the service felt like I'd just been given parole!"—a feeling with which he would later become familiar indeed.

Screaming "At last" under his breath, Harry bolted down the aisle and headed for the great outdoors. Within a few minutes, with tie off and sleeves rolled up, Harry was playing with his young cousins at the monthly church dinner on the grounds. These were great moments in his life, giving him a certain sense of security that he derived from being part of a large family.

Plywood set across wood sawhorses served as tables for the picnic-style family meal. It was then time for a moment of prayer. All heads were bowed and eyes closed, with the exception of young Harry, whose eyes were transfixed on his grandmother, the visiting missionary, as she murmured her blessing over the food. Then the semi-controlled free-for-all began. Harry's eyes scanned the long table as he fixed his gaze on a large ham, plate of roast beef, mounds of potatoes, a pyramid of stacked corn on the cob, and other vegetables grown in the Greene garden. Harry ate his single obligatory string bean, while keeping his eyes focused on a smaller table where homemade cakes and pies were covered in netting. At the end of the meal, several of the women, including Harry's mother, brought out the desserts that had been refrigerated, including the lemon meringue pie and homemade ice cream made with rock salt. It was a day to remember.

These were great moments in his life, giving him a certain sense of security that he derived from being part of a large family.

As evening approached, the red-orange Tennessee sun silhouetted the corn stalks while the men sat on the porch smoking their pipes, cigars, and cigarettes. This was tobacco country. No thoughts in the fifties of lung cancer or the need for filters to screen out the nicotine. Harry's father sat on the same swing his father had sat on years earlier. Things really hadn't much changed from father to son. However, within a decade, because of some of Harry's decisions, things would change dramatically—all for the worse.

Bill Greene loved his son, but he remained emotionally distant. He didn't know how to say *I love you.* Harry mostly remembers the experience of going behind the woodshed, where his dad would firmly apply the board of education to the seat of knowledge.

More-enjoyable experiences occurred when Harry's grandmother and he would take their occasional walks. "You know, Harry, I pray for you and Dennis every day," Baba would tell her beloved grandson, patting his head affectionately. "I really do, Harry, every single day." The affirmation from the person he loved so much gave young Harry a warm feeling he never forgot—even though he didn't have the foggiest idea what she meant. He just knew that Baba loved him. That was enough for him at that time of his life.

Harry was the all-American country boy, learning decent Southern values about family, church, and country.

In some ways, Harry's entire childhood was set in an idyllic world, not unlike the fantasy of a Disney screenplay. Harry was the all-American country boy, learning decent Southern values about family, church, and country. His summer days consisted of swinging from the big tree in the front yard, swimming in the fishing hole with his brother and cousins, and exploring the acres of hiding places for the nonstop cops-and-robbers game with his brother. Harry never once wanted for food, clothes, or the warmth of an extended family—something he appreciated all the more when the once-energetic young boy suddenly found himself suffering from severe daily fatigue.

When his sickness was finally diagnosed, the doctors informed Harry's parents that their son had the dreaded rheumatic fever. Harry was forced to stay in bed for two months and put down as many as twenty aspirins a day. In later years, the residual nature of the illness would prevent him from participating in high school sports. Harry's mother allowed him to take part of his bed rest on the living room couch, where he and the rest of the family could watch their new thirteen-inch, black-and-white television. Just as in millions of other American homes, the Greene family's schedule began to revolve around popular television programs such as *Gunsmoke, Have Gun—Will Travel, The Rifleman*, and *Wagon Train*. Almost overnight, the Greenes paid no more attention to the large radio in the hall, now a relic that was gathering dust as the new world of television entertainment swept the family away into nightly worlds of fantasy and action.

Soon Harry's health improved—an answer to prayer, insisted the family. Harry's family had now pulled up stakes and moved to Knoxville, and the following year, Baba returned from her missionary work in Alaska to manage the first Christian bookstore in the state of Virginia, a Southern Baptist enterprise located in downtown Roanoke. A year later, she moved on to manage Wills Book Store in Greensboro, North Carolina—a place Harry would frequent whenever possible. Harry had become an avid reader, but he wasn't all that fond of Christian biographies. Harry remembers, "I thought of them as no more than stories of dead people. Christian leaders and Christian subjects were irrelevant to me. Sure, I kept getting perfect attendance records in Sunday school, but the living God had no place in my heart. I was more fascinated with walking through the stacks of printed books of Wills Book

Store, enjoying the smell of fresh paper and ink. But the things of God? Well, they just weren't for me."

However, Harry would do just about anything to please his beloved grandmother, so that summer, at twelve years of age, he signed up to attend the Eagle Eyre Camp near Lynchburg, Virginia, where Baba was responsible for a book display. Harry remembers one day how the youth speaker gave an impassioned evangelistic invitation for the children to come to know Jesus Christ. As he spoke, Baba's eyes riveted on young Harry. Harry felt her presence and, he recalls, "I made the decision to walk forward toward the makeshift altar. As I did, I glanced back to see the excitement and glow on my grandmother's face. I had freely said the words, 'I trust Christ for my salvation, and I take Him as my Savior,' but that's all they were. Just words. I spoke them only to please my grandmother. There was not a single part of my being that believed in God, Jesus Christ, or anything else religious. I was, however, beginning to believe in Harry."

> **"There was not a single part of my being that believed in God, Jesus Christ, or anything else religious. I was, however, beginning to believe in Harry."**

Unable to control her delight in Harry's decision, Grandma Sullivan could hardly wait to share the good news with Harry's parents. "He's born again, he's saved. Praise the Lord," she said to Maggie Mae on the phone. Baba then embraced Harry and whispered that one day the Lord would use him mightily for the cause of Christ. Harry remembers, "It felt good to make my grandmother so happy, and I can still see the joy in her eyes—even after all these years. I don't know if it was the first time I realized that I had the ability to con people, but I certainly now recognized that I had the *power* to do it—to do it well, and to do it whenever I felt like it. Such a skill would not serve me well in the days to follow."

At age thirteen Harry was baptized. The pastor, Dr. Wade Bryant, carefully wrapped his hand with a handkerchief to cover Harry's nose and mouth, and quickly dipped the growing boy backward into the four-foot-deep church tank as Harry's choir robe floated on the surface. As he slowly found his way out of the water, Harry was more concerned that the experience had messed up his hair than he was about his "new life" in Christ. Changing into his clothes in a room behind the church baptistery, he thought, *Funny, but I don't feel any different. All I know is that I walked in that tank dry, and I came out wet. What was the big deal?* It had been slowly incubating for months—perhaps years. Now, Harry's philosophy of hedonism and self-sufficiency was beginning to come to the surface. Confident that he was now able to rule his own world, he would say to himself, *I think I'm finally getting this thing figured out. If I can just play the game the right way—and long enough—life will get easier and easier for me, and, in the end, I will get more privileges.* Within a few years, however, his self-ingratiating attitude would send Harry on a downward spiral to the depths of physical, mental, and spiritual despair—and into the pit of hell itself.

Full Pardon

Harry's philosophy of *if I just play the game, life will be easier and easier, and I will get more privileges* is not uncommon among the thinking of the millions of inmates in our nation's jails and prisons today. A personal philosophy of self-interest, self-indulgence, and self-importance is only one of the ingredients that have put these prisoners behind bars. That's why our Good News chaplains faithfully enter the prison cells of male and female prisoners 365 days a year, sharing Jesus and His great love, listening to inmates' stories, and putting their arms of compassion about those who seem to have come to the end of the road.

Good News chaplains remember how Hosea spoke of God's love and forgiveness when the prophet said, "When Israel was a child, then I loved him, and called my son out of Egypt. As they called them, so they went from them: they sacrificed unto Ba'alim, and burned incense to graven images. I taught E'phraim also to go, taking them by their arms; but they knew not that I healed them. . . How shall I give thee up, E'phraim? how shall I deliver thee, Israel? . . . mine heart is turned within me, my repentings are kindled together" (Hosea 11:1–3, 8). This is the work of Good News Jail & Prison Ministry: our chaplains' love for Christ and for prisoners both at home and abroad is so strong that they will return tomorrow, and the next day, and then the next, ministering God's love to those who need a special touch from our Heavenly Father.

Chapter 4

Bad Choices

John was a bad boy, and beat a poor cat;
Tom put a stone in a blind man's hat;
James was the boy who neglected his prayers;
They've all grown up ugly, and nobody cares.
Nursery rhyme

Harry's family moved to Roanoke, Virginia, when he was in the seventh grade. That's when his choices started to worry them. Their son with the pins on his lapel designating perfect Sunday school attendance was beginning to forsake the hymns of the faith for the new, more primitive beat of Elvis Presley, Chubby Checker, and the Isley Brothers—throbbing sounds that now pulsated through the walls of the once relatively quiet Greene home. Harry's obsession with rock and roll, however, was more than a spectator activity. The music and its cadence energized the young teenager so much that he decided to study percussion. By age sixteen, Harry was lead drummer in a rock band and immensely popular with his classmates. The musical addition to Harry's life made him even more exciting to his friends—especially the girls who began to flock around the fledging musician. His broad, captivating smile, flashing blue eyes, brown hair, and solid physique didn't seem to hurt either.

There were other influences on Harry's life. His father was a great sports fan and desperately wanted his son to play football. Harry did play ball during his freshman year, but because of his earlier bout with rheumatic fever, the doctors would never allow him to play after that. Meanwhile, Harry continued to enjoy sports. The teenager's heroes were baseball players such as Roger Maris, Whitey Ford, and Mickey

Mantle—all New York Yankees. Harry remembers when his father once drove the five hours to Griffith Stadium in Washington, D.C., to watch the Washington Redskins play the Philadelphia Eagles. Harry doesn't remember much about that day with his father—except that it was cold and rainy.

Other than sports, it seemed that he and his father had little to talk about. Before long, the emotional distance between Harry and his father had become a chasm, with every attempt at conversation between the two invariably becoming a heated argument. "The basis for our quarrels was the fact that I was now earning more money than my father," Harry remembers. "At age sixteen, I was making $300 to $400 a week playing music in bars, while my father was only bringing in $250 as an insurance adjuster."

> ## "At age 16, I was making $300 to $400 a week playing music in bars, while my father was only bringing in $250 as an insurance adjuster."

Meanwhile, Harry followed the beat and drummed his way to popularity to the delight of his peers at William Fleming High School, a long brick building filled with pony tails and poodle skirts, crew cuts, duck tails, rolled-up sleeves and blue jeans, and hot rods. It would have been the perfect set for *American Graffiti*. But to Harry, education wasn't nearly as important as partying. Fast becoming the center of his own life, Harry enjoyed the attention of the girls and had no qualms about breaking the law on underage drinking. First it was beer, then vodka, and finally a real man's drink, bourbon, the beverage of choice of his movie hero, John Wayne, in *Rio Bravo* and *The High and the Mighty,* and the likes of Mickey Spillane and Zane Grey.

Harry began staying out late every night of the week, a newfound freedom largely made possible because of one major purchase—a '58 Plymouth Fury—sharp, flashy, and much larger than his father's automobile, something that created even more quarrels and competition with his father. Harry's primary retreat from the conflict with his dad was his beloved rock and roll. Once he had bought his car, he had less reason to stay home and more freedom to play in places such as Pappa Joe's, Johnny's, the Brook Club, and other dance halls in the area. Harry was good, and the pulsating rhythm of his bass, snare, and cymbals kept couples dancing well past midnight. Fast becoming a legend in his own mind—and with enough cash in his pockets to treat his friends to dinner and drink as if there were no tomorrow— Harry figured he had it made. He loved to hold court with "King Harry" seated on the throne. He loved the attention and the approval. The more affirmation he received, the more he wanted—and needed.

If Harry had ever worn all his Sunday school attendance medals at one time, he might have been mistaken for a young general. But by the time he was seventeen, the shiny gold pins had now been pushed to the back of the drawer—out of sight and out of mind. Weary of memorizing any more Bible verses to please his family and church officials, and refusing to do the "Sunday school thing" any longer, Harry mentally packed up any desire to follow the things of God—Someone he no longer believed in. One day Harry said to a friend, "This whole religious thing is bogus. Besides, nothing some dead Jew did two thousand years ago could possibly affect me."

If Harry had a passion for rock and roll, he was equally consumed with his physical appearance. His hair was neatly cut in a Troy Donahue-style flattop, the fad of the early sixties. His money went for expensive dress shirts, chino pants, and white bucks, all of which he wore to class with pride.

Full Pardon

Harry was becoming a fine drummer indeed, and he was getting better with every passing day. His musical success, punctuated by the encouragement of his peers, soon made Harry think that a career of playing with bigger bands in bigger clubs—with perhaps lucrative record contracts—were viable options. Meanwhile, Harry drummed on, king of the dance hall, with money in his pockets and more friends than he knew what to do with.

The year was now 1961—his senior year of high school—and all his teachers and classmates assumed that Harry would go on to college. His senior yearbook was filled with glowing inscriptions, such as "nice guy," "good friend," "cute," and "talented" from his friends. Teachers wrote, "hard worker," "popular," and, to complete the glowing image of the all-American boy image, "patriotic." Even though Harry was more concerned with himself than others, there were a few whom he respected. One was John Glenn, who was the first American to orbit the earth. Harry was impressed by his great accomplishment—especially because this brave astronaut was also a military man. Still, Harry did not feel he had a role model worthy of following. The Oscar for Best Picture that year went to *Lawrence of Arabia,* a film Harry hated because he saw Lawrence as a distinct feminine figure, anything but heroic. His real heroes were men such as Spartacus, Ben Hur, and, of course, the film legend John Wayne. He related to the toughness of soldiers and the smells of battle, and could see himself one day commanding great battalions in far-flung battlefields of the world. With the military a part of his family's past, Harry knew one day that he would end up serving his country in some capacity.

Shortly after graduation, Harry discovered through a friend (whose father was on the local draft board) that his number was high, which meant there was a good chance he could be drafted and sent to Vietnam. Harry decided to enlist in the Army so he could exert some control over where he might serve. He joined the Army with the promise that once enlisted he'd be able to play in the Army band. The young musician would rather beat on his drums than beat up on the enemy. Patriots, he figured, came in all sizes and attitudes.

Before long his music objectives were moving full speed ahead—until a freak accident happened. While Harry was in basic training at Fort Jackson, South Carolina, a floor buffer ran over his foot. The foot became badly infected and demanded a hospital stay. This unexpected medical emergency kept Harry from graduating with his basic training class, which meant he had to forfeit his opportunity to join the Army band. His next duty assignment was Advanced Infantry Training, again at Fort Jackson. While in AIT, Harry was offered the opportunity to be transferred to Fort Meyer, Virginia, and be assigned to the Old Guard honor guard. This was the group that handled all Arlington Cemetery burials, walked guard at the Tomb of the Unknowns, and assisted in other ceremonial duties in Washington. Harry had lucked out.

The ceremonial duties and the daily firing of rifles into the air soon became old hat, and Harry's mind began to fill with more demanding career possibilities. He thought it was time to see the world.

Upon his arrival at Fort Meyer, however, Harry was told he was too tall to be considered for duty at the Tomb of the Unknowns. That left him involved only in the ceremonial duties of the Old Guard, specifically in burial detail. While he performed his duties as a good soldier, increasingly he found his assignment boring, though he could not help but be moved by the caskets of dead soldiers returning from Vietnam to be buried in Arlington. The ceremonial duties and the daily firing of rifles into the air soon became old hat, and Harry's mind began to fill with more demanding career possibilities. He thought it was time to see the world—and what better way to see it than by volunteering to serve his country overseas. So Harry asked for a transfer to Germany.

Upon his arrival in West Berlin, he was immediately assigned as driver for the company's Executive Officer. At least he wasn't in Saigon, he figured. Harry arrived in Berlin deep inside East Germany in early 1963. Coming from a family of war heroes, Harry was not surprised when he soon began receiving awards such as Soldier of the Week and Brigade Soldier of the Month. Military recognition ran deep among his ancestors, and Harry was simply continuing a cherished family tradition.

The sight of "the wall" was a sobering experience to the nineteen-year-old soldier: concrete, twelve feet high, and three to four feet thick; 103 miles in length with 295 watch towers. In addition to the controlling presence of the Russian military, the East German police, known as the Stazi, had teams of angry dogs that patrolled no-man's-land, a one-hundred-meter-wide corridor. Anyone discovered in that area was shot immediately. On the top of the wall were miles of barbed wire and shards of sharp, broken glass. Harry remembers one day seeing the bodies of five men and women hanging on the jagged wire, left there to rot. As evening approached, the killing zone would suddenly take on an unearthly feeling as searchlights scanned the area, dogs barked ferociously, and the communist military spent the night poking rods into the dirt in search of tunnels.

For the most part, he liked his job; what he didn't like was sitting out those long, boring hours in the command post with only water to drink and K rations to eat. As he would peer long distances through his binoculars, he could see the machine guns of the enemy trained directly at him and his fellow soldiers. Harry admits there were a few times while in Berlin when he wished he were back at Fort Meyer in the Old Guard. He knew if the Cold War ever were to escalate into actual combat that East Germany was not the place to be. But he had volunteered to be here, and here he was—without any other exciting career options currently available, or so he thought.

Even though he carried out his obligations as a good soldier, it was hardly all work and no play. When off duty, Harry lost himself wenching and carousing in the debauchery of the wild, promiscuous nightlife of West Berlin, where he drank with the best and worst of his fellow soldiers, downing inordinate amounts of liquor night after night.

Harry figured, "Hey, you there, in the mirror . . . you should be giving orders, not taking them."

Harry recalls, "I was drinking like a fish, and party time usually meant all-night sex." In fact, the more fun he had off duty, the more tired he grew of his dull military routine. One day Harry remembers standing in front of a mirror where he imagined himself in full-dress uniform wearing the insignias of a general. He liked what he "saw." "'Hey, you there, in the mirror, you—General Greene—you should be giving orders, not taking them.'" Oddly, he was actually standing alone in a barracks latrine, an unseemly venue for announcing such lofty career goals. Shortly after, Harry appeared before his company commander questioning him on how he might become an officer. His CO told him there were two choices: he could apply either for West Point Military Academy or Officer Candidate School. The thought of Harry Greene, West Point Cadet, appealed to his ego, and he chose to set off on that course. He went before two review boards made up of officers who were ranked Major and higher and was unanimously approved for transfer back to the United States for entry into the U.S. Military Academy Preparatory School at Fort Belvoir, Virginia, just south of the nation's capital.

Harry says, "I remember writing to my parents, 'One day there will be another General Greene in the family, and I will be the man.'" In September 1963, with that promise to his parents firmly in his mind, the young solider began his preparatory training.

However, reality suddenly caught up with the young soldier. Harry's high school social life and his passion to become the best drummer alive had kept him from engaging in serious academic work. Now, surprise, surprise, his instructors were more interested in substance than shadow. He tried to schmooze his way through prep school, but this time the golden boy's charm was not enough to compensate for his less-than-brilliant scholarship. During the first six weeks, he failed two out of three tests. Math was his worst. "Greene," said the Commanding Officer, calling Harry into his office one day, "You're taking up space here, son. There are plenty of people who are willing to work hard to be here, but it's obvious you're not one of those people. You're being placed back on active duty, and we're transferring you to Alaska."

Alaska? The place where his grandmother had done her mission work? Cold, remote Alaska? No, not Alaska. Harry recalls, "I found being banished to Alaska too extreme a punishment for only failing a couple tests. It dashed my hopes of going to West Point, and it ruined my carefully made plans of becoming an officer." Until now, things had always come relatively easy for Harry: he had never suffered a major disappointment that proved to be a serious problem, always figuring his charisma, good looks, and bravado would see him through. And it did, up until now. Suddenly, big, brash Harry hit a wall, and his response to rejection would now unleash a series of options, among them some of the worst choices he would ever make. Harry says, "I was angry and hurt. I felt like the Army hadn't really given me the chance I deserved. It wasn't fair to cut me loose like that. And Alaska? That was cruel and unusual punishment." But fair or not, reality was that Harry had flunked out, and now he felt humiliated. Becoming "General Greene" just wasn't going to happen.

**Fair or not, reality was
that Harry had flunked out,
and now he felt humiliated.**

After being summarily dismissed from his brief sojourn at prep school, Harry returned to his home near Knoxville. His parents were delighted to see their "little general," who had arrived by bus in full military uniform. He had been given thirty days to report for duty in Alaska. While displaying an outward calm, Harry kept his darkest thoughts a secret. He had decided to go AWOL—absence without leave. He'd simply walk away, deserting his military responsibilities.

Harry found himself at home on November 22, 1963, when a bulletin broke on the television screen that announced the assassination of President John F. Kennedy. Harry looked at the TV and heard Walter Cronkite say, "This just in. President Kennedy has been shot. At 12:30 P.M. the president was struck by two rifle bullets, one at the base of his neck and one in the head. He was dead upon arrival at Parkland Memorial Hospital in Dallas." Harry had seen the president twice: once up close, and once from a distance. Although he had already made the decision to go AWOL, Harry was still a patriot, and this was the assassination of *his* commander in chief. As the awareness of the death of JFK hit home, Harry felt more anger than sadness.

Full Pardon

Two days after Kennedy's funeral, Harry arrived in Washington, D.C., where he took refuge in a cheap hotel on the corner of 14th and K streets. The rate was five dollars a night—about all he could afford. There, he removed his uniform, vowing never to wear it again. He was still on his thirty-day leave and had plenty of time to change his mind about going AWOL—something he considered seriously at first. However, at the end of those thirty days, he determined to stay the crooked course he had chosen. He also had one other pressing problem: *he was running out of cash*. Harry refused to return home to ask his parents for money, mainly because he knew it would be only a matter of days before Army authorities would contact his folks to inform them their son had not returned to active duty. But the money was now vanishing fast, and he was tired of his low life in cheap hotels. He knew he had to be creative. Fast.

"I didn't have the courage to go back and face the music," Harry says. "If I had returned to the Army and confessed to my AWOL, at worst I probably would only have received stockade time. And with my good record—and playing the victim to my 'disappointment' with prep school and all that—I probably would only have received a slap on the wrist or a reduction in rank. But I decided that I wasn't going to do that. I had already begun to make plans for another, more exciting, way to live— and to make lots of money in the process. That's when I made one of the worst decisions of my life. *I decided to start writing bad checks.*"

Harry knew he would obviously be breaking the law, but he figured he was clever enough to carry out his crime. After all, it would only be a *little* crime. Harry remembers the day he decided to do the deed: "I convinced myself that if I wrote a bad check for only $25 it would be all right," Harry says. "So I took out a checkbook from an account I'd opened before I went to Germany—when I'd been at Fort Meyer—and put my little plan into operation. I convinced myself that the check would only be for $25 to buy food at a grocery store, so what harm could there be in that? I rationalized. That was the precise moment I became like a lot of the people I was about to meet—men and women who also had set the parameters of 'I know this is wrong, but it's just slightly wrong.' The problem with that kind of thinking is that once you do the 'slightly wrong,' then you move quickly to the 'well, it's not really too wrong,' and then to the 'very wrong.' That's what happened to me."

Harry's next bad check limit was fifty dollars, and then there was no limit. Before long, he was going into banks and opening up as many accounts as possible—most for as little as ten dollars—and walking out with a handful of blank checks. That little crime spree put Harry over the top fast, or so he thought. For six months—working eight checkbooks from eight separate banks—he was living higher on the hog than he'd ever lived before. He spent most of the money recklessly, but on occasion he'd make a creative "investment." Harry would write bad checks for things such as $2,500 worth of television sets and then sell them to a "fence" to help boost his resources. Young Harry Greene was in business.

> **"The problem with that kind of thinking is that once you do the 'slightly wrong,' then you move quickly to the 'well, it's not really too wrong,' and then to the 'very wrong.' That's what happened to me."**

Money was now flowing like water into Harry's pockets, and with the dramatic improvement of his personal finances, Harry rationalized he really deserved to stay in some of the finer hotels, places such as the exclusive Shoreham in

Washington, D.C. It was 1964, and Harry was able to pay one hundred dollars a night or more for lodging. He would check in with as many as eight designer suits, a Rolex watch, bracelets, and solid gold cufflinks. Officially, Harry's crimes were forgery and grand larceny—the easiest money he'd ever made. But like any addict refusing to come off his "high," Harry had to have more, which meant he became bolder and bolder with his check-writing scam. He wouldn't and couldn't stop his wave of crime.

Meanwhile, the affable deserter was gathering a host of new friends—something not difficult to do when the money and booze are flowing freely. Harry recalls, "I got great personal pleasure in paying for large entertainment bills, such as a ringside table for the Tony Bennett show in a swank Washington, D.C., night club, or picking up the restaurant tab for a party of 'friends' with my stolen money. I remember sitting in smoke-filled lounges, impressing my friends with the city's best nightlife, and listening to the stars of the music world of that era. It was great fun—while it lasted."

And it just kept getting better, or so Harry thought. With his lifestyle now on the upswing, the young con moved into a five-star hotel, where he paid hundreds of dollars a night; this, of course, demanded that he acquire even larger sums of money. For the first time, Harry had thousands of dollars in his pockets. He was brash and bold as a person, and that's also how he was becoming in his crimes. Harry remembers, "I'd actually go back to the same stores again and again, writing bad checks, as if I were invincible, actually enjoying the thrill of committing crimes—and the high that came from not getting caught." Here was a twenty-year-old living the high life who was conning to live, and living to con, all the time thinking he'd devised the perfect plan.

Harry vividly remembers one of his more creative cons: "When I would check into a five-star hotel, I'd ask the desk clerk to put $1,000 of my cash in the safe. During the next few nights, I would then withdraw most of my money—while another clerk was on duty, of course—and after one or two weeks, I'd use the fire escape or go over the wall, leaving the hotel with thousands of dollars in unpaid bills. Sure, I realized I might get caught one day, but being intoxicated by the presence of so many 'friends' and having so much money, I really didn't give it too much thought."

It was easy to get false IDs in Washington, D.C.; it was just as convenient to hang out with the criminal element in the city. So Harry began to develop friendships with the desperate and the notorious in the bars, clubs, and lounges of the city. He had the cash and he had the flash. One day he befriended two other felons named John and Donnie: John was an old-time con from the West Coast, someone Harry didn't really trust, but he found the relationship, well, adventuresome. Donnie was Harry's age—all of twenty years—and had already served time in state prison. The new relationships quickly became the beginning of yet another downward spiral in Harry's life.

In those days, however, everything Harry did was on or over the edge. His pattern of deceit even extended to his relationship with women. Harry admits, "I was living with one girl on the weekends and another one on weekdays. I know that was pretty risky, but fortunately for me, they didn't know each other. More than once I hoped it would stay that way. My life was good indeed: wine, women, song, money, jewelry, and the finest clothes a person could buy."

One day, without much thought, Harry found himself with John and Donnie planning a bold armed robbery. They had obtained two .38 revolvers and a .45-caliber pistol in preparation for their crime. Their target: a Washington, D.C., Safeway store the following Friday evening, where payroll checks could be cashed, and where there would be tens of

Full Pardon

thousands of dollars waiting for them. Harry recognized that he'd upped the ante this time and that the idea of pulling a robbery was something he'd never entertained before. He had enjoyed firing weapons while in the military, but now he realized he was moving into a higher, more lethal league, one with the prospect of shooting, if not killing, innocent people, during an armed robbery. Philosophers remind us that *today's decision always becomes tomorrow's reality*. Harry, however, was hardly in a philosophical mood. In his hardening criminal heart, *he had no doubt that he could commit murder.*

He had enjoyed firing weapons while in the military, but now he realized he was moving into a higher, more lethal league, one with the prospect of shooting, if not killing, innocent people.

Murderers. Rapists. Thieves. Con artists. Our nation's jail and prison cells are filled with the kinds of people young Harry Greene was fast becoming. In fact, in the United States today, if crime were tied to a twenty-four-hour clock representing the annual ratio of crime to fixed time intervals, the results would be:

- One murder committed every twenty-two seconds

- One woman raped every five minutes

- One robbery committed every forty-seven seconds

- One aggravated assault committed every twenty-eight seconds

- One violent crime committed every twenty-two seconds

- One automobile stolen every twenty seconds

- One burglary committed every eleven seconds

- One crime against property committed every three seconds

And into this world of pain, hate, and godless confusion come our Good News chaplains, who minister daily to those who have been apprehended for their crimes against society. With the power of a living God, these chaplains are committed to helping break the cycle of crime—one life at a time. The refreshing, good news is that together, we *can* break this cycle of crime one life at a time!

Chapter 5

"Mr. Greene, It's Over"

It is good for me that I have been afflicted;
that I might learn thy statutes.
Psalm 119:71

Harry was driving the streets of Alexandria, Virginia, in a rented black Cadillac heading to a steak house in Washington, D.C., for dinner with several of his friends. It was 7 P.M. on June 10, 1964. Suddenly Harry spotted some flashing red lights following closely behind him. The police car was gaining speed. With pulse quickening and heart racing, Harry wondered if this would be a routine traffic stop, since he was traveling 45 m.p.h. in a 30 m.p.h. zone. Or might it be something worse? Either way, Harry had already decided what he would do after being stopped—he would resist any attempt at arrest. Harry pulled over to the curb and the officer exited his patrol car, walking slowly toward the Cadillac. Harry's mind was working fast now. He knew what he had to do; it would now only be a matter of split-second timing.

With his mind spinning, he purposely left the engine running, prepared at a moment's notice to stomp on the accelerator and make his escape. As the officer approached the car, Harry watched him carefully through his rearview mirror, right foot still ready to step on the gas. But Harry failed to see that another police car had just pulled in front of him, effectively blocking the Cadillac from any possible means of flight. Harry knew that this was no simple traffic stop. The officer finally arrived at the door to Harry's car, saying, "It's over, Mr. Greene. Get out of the car with your hands raised." Harry slumped, and with no prospect of a quick getaway, he turned off the engine.

Harry recalls the moment: "I think back now and ask myself, *What if I'd been in possession of the .45 handgun I was planning to use for the robbery? Then what would have happened? A shoot-out? Would I have killed a cop?* Possibly. I know I might have engaged in some act of violence, because I was so angry for getting caught. Fortunately for all parties involved, the gun was with my two partners, since it was still two days before the robbery. I think God—in whom I still had no trust—might have been saying to me, *Harry, I'm not going to let you do it. I have a plan for your life and it does not include your carrying out an armed robbery. So, you'll be arrested tonight.* And arrested I was—two days before the planned armed robbery. I now know beyond the shadow of a doubt that the hand of God was on my life."

"'Harry, I'm not going to let you do it. I have a plan for your life and it does not include your carrying out an armed robbery. So, you'll be arrested tonight.'"

You'll remember how Harry already had admitted to enjoying the companionship of two women at the same time—one on weekends, and one during the week—and how he had always hoped they would never discover the liaison. Well, unfortunately for Harry, it didn't work out as he had hoped. "One of the girls I was living with found out about my relationship with her competition across town, and she quickly put two and two together," Harry says. "That's when she decided to go to the police and tell them everything she knew about me. 'Yeah, we've got a warrant for Mr. Greene's arrest,' said the police officer on duty. At that moment, unknown to me at the time, my fate was sealed. My girlfriend gave the police the make, model, and license number of the car I was driving, and that was it. I was arrested right there on the spot."

A crowd began to gather on the sidewalk to see what the police cars and flashing red lights were all about. "Spread out over the hood!" one officer shouted. The police searched Harry's pockets, frisked him, and brought his hands behind his back. For the first time in his life Harry felt the cold, hard metal of handcuffs as he stood helplessly spread eagle over the hood of his car. He could hear the sound and feel the tightening of the cuffs as they pressed hard into his thick wrists—something he would hear and feel often in the months to follow.

Strangely, the arrest brought Harry a sense of relief as the heavy weight of running from the law had finally fallen from his broad shoulders. He'd been carrying his guilt for too long, living the life of a fugitive, hanging on the edge, always watching his back. Now the words "Mr. Greene, it's over" had brought him to his knees and to his senses. Harry recalls, "Within minutes, I was unceremoniously escorted by police car to the Alexandria jail. I remember sitting silently in the rear seat of that patrol car, looking out of the window at sights familiar to me—but this time with one critical difference: I was no longer a free man. Within minutes, I was booked at the Alexandria jail, and then transferred immediately to Arlington, where there was a previous warrant for my arrest. My designer suits, jewelry, and the thousands of dollars I'd stashed in the hotel safe wouldn't be of much use to me that night."

Harry's new home was now Cell Block C. Once he'd been booked and had settled in, one of the first things he did was to make a collect call to his parents from a phone hanging on the jail wall. His mother answered.

"'Mom, this is Harry," he said.

Before she had a chance to say anything, he added, "I'm in a lot of trouble. I really screwed up."

"Where are you?" she asked.

"I'm in jail," he answered, "but everything's fine."

"In jail? Whatever possessed you?" she asked. "Why are you putting us through this? And why didn't you call all these months?"

Harry could hardly wait to finish the conversation. "But everything's fine, Mom. I got a lawyer. Things will be okay." As he hung up the phone he could still hear his mother crying. He returned to his cell, where he would spend his new life with people he didn't like, eat food that was less than appetizing, and live out his uncertain days in an atmosphere he detested. *Welcome to life behind bars.*

Chaplain Simmer had to compete with loud conversations over card games, the harsh sounds of metal doors opening and closing, toilets flushing, occasional shouting, and a radio blaring in the background.

The next day Harry saw Chaplain Bill Simmer for the first time as the minister to prisoners arrived at the six cell blocks of the Arlington County Jail to carry out his work of listening and counseling. Some of the inmates regarded the chaplain as a good, decent guy, but since jail life is hardly conducive to things religious, there was little enthusiasm about his presence. Most of the time Chaplain Simmer had to compete with loud conversations over card games, the harsh sounds of metal doors opening and closing, toilets flushing, occasional shouting, and a radio blaring in the background. It was not an ideal ministry situation, since inmates would simply turn their backs on this man of the cloth, keep playing their games, and go on endlessly bragging about how they were the most accomplished burglar or car thief or whatever. Exaggeration was always the name of their game.

Harry quickly figured out that life in jail could either be lived, or it could be dragged out, so he determined to make the best of it. His style was to stay up all night and sleep during the day—a pattern that reflected much of his life before prison. This time, however, the one critical difference between "outside" and "inside" life was Chaplain Bill. Harry had long since quit going to church. After all, the things of God had become as remote to his thinking as the farthest planet. There had been no time for God on the outside, and there was certainly no place in his life for the Almighty now. In fact, Harry could hardly remember the last time he'd heard a Christian message. But now, here was Chaplain Bill, coming by day after day. Harry remembers the exact moment when Chaplain Bill tried to get a conversation going with him about spiritual things. Harry respectfully responded, "Look, you've got to understand that I don't believe in God, and I'm not religious. What I really *do* need, however, is a good lawyer." Chaplain Bill, Bible in hand, didn't press the issue, and moved on to talk with the other prisoners. But before he left to continue his witness, he turned quietly to Harry and said, "Any time you want to talk, I'll listen. I'll be here every day for you."

Meanwhile, Harry's rows of well-tailored suits, hanging in the closet of a five-star hotel several miles away, had now given way to a new form of attire—a rumpled, khaki jail uniform. Harry recalls his first impressions of his new home: "I didn't like anything about my surroundings, but the thing I hated most was being so restricted in space. I'm a pretty big guy, and I never liked boundaries in the first place. But this was the worst—a cell measuring eight by five by ten feet with a double bunk. I barely fit! And there was also something else I learned quickly, that living in jail is all about playing games and trying to figure out the guys we could manipulate the most. There were always one or two we could have our way with—even among the COs. But there was one person I didn't think anyone could manipulate: *me!*

Because of his size, most of Harry's fellow inmates tended to keep their distance. If they hadn't, he easily could have taken care of himself. "I learned that personal security wasn't a real issue for me," he says. "But I did learn that, as in any society—and prison is definitely a society—there are strict rules about not stealing from others or cheating at card games. To help enforce these laws, there was always a 'boss man' on the prowl—a leader who would do what he needed to do to assume control of the cell unit. A couple of times I was the designated boss. I guess it was actually the next step in the development of my leadership skills."

**"Harry, I'd like to give you a Bible."
Harry looked at the chaplain in disbelief.
"A Bible? Now why would I want a Bible?"
he sarcastically replied, turning down
Chaplain Bill's request.**

Meanwhile, Chaplain Bill Simmer kept spending time at Cell Block C. Friendly, non-pushy, and happy to talk to inmates about everything from sports to cars to the headlines of the day, Chaplain Bill just kept showing up. One day he sought out Harry and said, "Harry, I'd like to give you a Bible." Harry looked at the chaplain in disbelief. "A Bible? Now why would I want a Bible?" he sarcastically replied, turning down Chaplain Bill's request. But never being one to take no for an answer, especially when he stood before a captive audience, Chaplain Bill returned the very next day and asked Harry if he wanted to join a Bible study. Harry couldn't believe this guy. *What part of "no, thank you" did he not understand?* If Harry didn't want a copy of the Bible, why would he be interested in a Bible study? But the seasoned chaplain knew what he was doing, sensing all along that, over time, Harry could be reached with the message of Jesus Christ. In fact, on several occasions when Bill was sharing from the Scriptures or preaching to the inmates in their cells, he observed Harry lying on his bunk reading a book. Trouble was, the book he was reading was often upside down, which, to even the most careless observer, might just indicate that Harry was listening to the chaplain's message more attentively than he was prepared to admit.

Harry was an arrogant prisoner, settling into his new jail life in a strangely comfortable way. But even with all his bravado about being so tough and not believing in God, Harry started to have second thoughts about the ever-present Chaplain Bill. Harry would overhear him talking to other inmates about current events, or sports, or cars, or the news of the day, and he could tell his fellow prisoners were actually enjoying their relationship with the chaplain. Bill had this uncanny gift of beginning a conversation with something subtle, and then sensitively turning the subject to spiritual matters without an inmate even realizing what he was doing. The toughest inmates, even those who wanted nothing to do with Bill Simmer's message, were continually amazed at his dedication and persistence—and at his compassion for them and their condition. It was obvious that Chaplain Bill Simmer loved his Lord and that he loved his ministry to prisoners. That love was not lost on young Harry Greene.

"Chaplain Bill was always friendly to me every time he came by the cell block," Harry remembers. "I hated to admit it at the time, but Bill's presence was more positive than anything I'd experienced in a very long time. He really was an interesting guy—and he also knew exactly what interested us prisoners. I think back on how he would bring in his sixteen-millimeter projector and set it up in the middle of the cell block, where he would show us his inventory of Moody Science Films. Like most of the other inmates, I would watch those film sessions mostly because it broke my dull routine. For an hour or so, I could get my mind off the 'zoo' I was living in."

As he sat on his jail bunk bed, he began to realize that in no way was he in control of his own life. The thought was devastating.

One day Harry viewed the popular Moody film *City of the Bees*, a powerful, dramatic scientific presentation that also told the story of God's boundless love. After the film was over, Bill tried to get a few words in with Harry about his relationship to God, but all the young inmate wanted to do was argue. Chaplain Simmer wouldn't take the bait, and instead came back to Harry with another Scripture, and another, and yet another. Harry became so angry that he returned to his cell. But as he sat on his jail bunk bed, he began to realize that in no way was he in control of his own life. The thought was devastating.

Harry always kept his back to the cell block wall because he knew he lived among people whose own lives were a mixture of turmoil and paranoia. He quickly learned whom he could trust and whom he couldn't. He also loved to read, and he spent most of his time turning the pages of mystery novels—his own way of attempting to escape the reality of his surroundings. But the one reality he could not escape was the constant presence of Chaplain Bill. Harry recalls, "In a sense, Bill put me off because I felt he wasn't trying hard enough to convert me. He wasn't twisting my arm, forcing me to read the Bible or demanding that I attend one of his Bible studies. Suddenly, I realized I was running out of excuses. One day Chaplain Simmer said to me, 'Harry, think about it. Jesus Christ is either the Son of God or He is the greatest liar the world has ever known.' His words got me thinking, even though I did my best to block them out and shut them off."

From Chaplain Simmer's perspective, Harry's basic problem was pride. Harry never thought of himself as a criminal, Bill would later say, nor did he ever believe he deserved to be locked up with those other ne'er-do-wells. Harry figured he was a cut above the rest of his fellow inmates, and the last thing he wanted was to follow the counsel of a chaplain. Only weak people needed religion for a crutch, Harry figured. Pushing God and the chaplain aside, Harry stayed consumed with two things: smoking and gambling. It was all he had to live for.

One day Harry stood in front of a polished piece of metal, which substituted for a mirror in his cell block. "I looked into that metal and immediately imagined myself dressed in full uniform, standing erect, and wearing the insignias of a general. But instead of a military uniform, all I could see was jailhouse khaki. That's when I sensed a strange feeling come over me, one of desperation, as I saw myself as I really was—a prisoner in an ugly brown uniform, the clothing of a caged animal in human form. Life was not supposed to turn out this way for me—Harry Greene, the great drummer, would-be general, and future American military hero."

Harry's grandmother continued to pray for him. She wrote him long letters of love and encouragement that said she would never stop loving him. She wanted so much to visit her grandson, but Harry knew he could never face her; he had too much inner shame. So the visit never happened.

Meanwhile, Chaplain Bill knew there had to be a crack in Harry's stubborn veneer somewhere, although he did not yet know what it was. Whatever his vulnerability might be, Harry refused to show it to Bill. He continued to stonewall this chaplain, who truly cared about his eternal soul. But the emotional barriers Harry erected between himself and the chaplain didn't seem to bother Bill. He just kept returning to Cell Block C day after day, standing on the other side of the bars, preaching the love of God to the inmates—even when it seemed as if no one was listening.

> **"Life was not supposed to turn out this way for me—Harry Greene, the great drummer, would-be general, and future American military hero."**

It was Sunday, October 11, 1964, and Harry was sitting on the floor of the cell block playing pinochle, as was his daily custom. The jail radio was intermittently blaring. One inmate was taking a shower. A few others were sleeping, and some were writings letters to loved ones. Chaplain Simmer had been preaching for about ten minutes when he suddenly read one verse from the Old Testament that caught Harry's attention. Bill read dramatically from Proverbs 14:12: "There is a way which seemeth right unto a man, but the end thereof are the ways of death." No one seemed to pay any attention to Chaplain Simmer as he preached that day—no one, that is, except Harry. The verse hammered into his mind! It was both inexplicable and surreal to the young prisoner as he got up, walked to the table, and sat down to listen to Bill.

To this day, Harry cannot remember the rest of the message Bill was preaching. Proverbs 14:12 was his focal point, and it is all he remembers. When Bill was finished, Harry told him, "I don't understand why, but that verse really caused me to think. I'd like to talk to you in private." Somehow, through all the noise and distraction, the young prisoner had heard Bill's voice proclaiming the good news that God loved people like Harry Greene. Harry says, "It was as if God reached down, thumped me on the head, and said, 'Hey, dummy, listen to this.'"

Bill told Harry that he had to speak to the men in the other cell blocks that morning, but assured him he would come by and talk to him the next day. True to his word, Bill came the next day to see Harry, and for the next two days Harry asked Bill questions, which the chaplain patiently answered, using only passages from God's Word.

Upon returning to his cell after talking with the chaplain, Harry finally admitted to himself that he alone was responsible for where he was. "I was living like an animal in a zoo because of what I had done," Harry says. "I looked at the food slot, and realized that I was being fed like an animal because I had committed numerous crimes. I admitted, finally, that I had chosen to break the law. Nobody but me was responsible for me being in jail."

After the third day of talking with Chaplain Bill, Harry suddenly ran out of questions. Harry explains, "I didn't want to believe. At the same time, I had no choice but to deal with what Bill kept telling me, that *I must either assume Jesus was the greatest liar in all of history, or I needed to accept Him at His word as the true Son of God.* Well, that day of personal decision finally became a reality. I can still see where Bill and I sat together in a solitary confinement cell, just off the jail's laundry room, one of the only 'private' places in the facility. Chaplain Simmer sat on the floor, with his back against the bars, while I sat on the edge of a toilet."

Full Pardon

In that less-than-auspicious location, Harry asked Jesus Christ to become his Savior and Lord—a moment in time that brought immediate peace to his rebellious, troubled heart. The Lord came into Harry's life, and he would never be the same again.

Harry Greene's story is just one of thousands in which the Spirit of the living God has invaded hearts of stone and made them tender through a relationship with the risen Lord. This is also true for those inmates who know Christ before they went to prison, as we read in this man's testimony:

"It was a Good News chaplain's encouragement that enabled me to withstand my stay in jail. Since I was a believer, I thought I knew what it meant to be a Christian before I went to jail. Eventually, I realized that I needed a stronger relationship with Christ.

"The chaplain encouraged me to cast my cares upon the Lord, study the Word, and pray. I became more humble as I grew in God's Word. I began to see how important my relationship with Jesus Christ was once I truly turned to Him in faithfulness. It is through this relationship that a person truly changes, regardless of his age. The key is a willingness to change and trust in Christ. Because of the caring of a Good News chaplain, God has given me an undivided heart."

Chapter 6

Chaplain Bill Was Always There

Nothing but Christ himself, your lord and
friend and brother, not all the doctrines about
him, even if they were true, can save you.
George MacDonald

There is power in the Word of God, and Proverbs 14:12,
which reads, "There is a way which seemeth right unto a
man, but the end thereof are the ways of death," kept ham-
mering Harry's mind. The more he heard that verse, the
more Harry came to realize three important things about his
life. "First, I knew I was not raised to be where I was at the
moment—in jail," he says. "Second, I knew I would never choose
to associate with these people on the outside. And third, I knew
in my heart there had to be something far better available to me
than what I was calling a life, which was really no life at all. I
was simply existing from day to day, moment to moment. That's
why I finally put down my playing cards and for the first time
really listened to what Chaplain Bill had to say."

On that Sunday when Harry asked him if they could talk,
Bill said, "Yes, of course, Harry, I'll be back tomorrow." True to
his word, Bill returned the next day. These many years later,
Harry reflects, "What I know now, but didn't fully understand
then, is that the chaplains are always there to help. It's not a
hit-or-miss proposition with them. You can always count on
them showing up—rain or shine, sleet or snow. That's because
the jail is their pulpit, and their congregations are those who
sit idly day after day in their cells and cell blocks—whether in
a dorm-style jail or in solitary confinement. The chaplain is
always there to establish relationships, to engage in both

meaningful and sometimes seemingly meaningless dialog with the inmates, and to answer questions, hoping that at some point in the conversation they will be able to turn the subject to spiritual things."

"When I realized how much he respected me as an individual, something happened inside. I felt worthy. Bill never once looked down on me for what I'd done; he didn't criticize me."

Harry was surprised that the chaplain showed such regard for the inmates as human beings. "When I realized how much he respected me as an individual, something happened inside," he says. "I began to feel worthy. Bill never once looked down on me for what I'd done; he didn't criticize me. There was neither rebuke in his face nor in his heart." Harry would later learn that rebuking is not the job of a chaplain. Instead, his assignment is to tell inmates of God's plan for their life, which includes a vital, personal relationship with Christ. And that's the message Bill was sharing with Harry.

Harry confesses, "For all those months of internal mutiny against God and things Christian, I must have been Bill's worst nightmare. All I wanted to do was argue. I was the smart, young, 'I've got all the answers,' 'I've been there,' 'I know this,' and, 'I've already memorized the Scripture' rebel. At first my whole thing was, 'This can't be right. I'm just getting emotional. Surely this will pass.' Trouble was that the more questions I asked, the more I realized my life was in shambles. I now know one of the main reasons I was open to accepting Christ as my Savior was that Bill was never confrontational or combative in his presentation. He answered my questions with Scripture, even as he explained the plan of salvation endlessly. I think the hardest thing about that plan of salvation for me was its simplicity. I kept wondering, *How could anything so profound—and with such eternal implications—be so terribly simple?"* In the end, however, Harry sat in the solitary-confinement cell with Chaplain Bill, whom he had kept at arm's length for so long. Won over by love, Harry was becoming ready to invite Jesus into his life.

Harry remembers how Bill looked him in the eye and said, "Why don't you accept Jesus Christ as your personal Savior? What's stopping you from doing that? Why won't you trust Christ to be your Savior and Lord?"

Harry answered, "I just can't believe it."

"Well, let me ask you this," said Bill. "Who was the first president of the United States?"

"George Washington, of course."

"Okay, tell me how you know that. Have you ever seen George Washington? Have you ever heard him? Have you ever talked to him?"

"Uh, no," Harry admitted.

"Well, then why do you believe that he was the first president of our country?"

"Well, I've read about him in my schoolbooks, and I've seen his picture, you know. I mean, we all know he was obviously our first president."

Bill wisely responded, "No, Harry, you believe all that about George Washington because *you choose to believe it.* Now, you need to choose to believe God. If you can believe in George Washington, you know you need to believe in God."

Harry looked at Bill and said, "I know you're right. But how do I do it?"

Bill simply said, "Let's pray," and while the chaplain and the inmate prayed, Harry Greene trusted Jesus as his Savior.

Meanwhile, the doors of the nearby cells were still slamming; prisoners were yelling and cursing at the COs. Yet, with all the noise and confusion of everyday jail life, Harry felt a peace he was hard-pressed to explain. Harry remembers, "My life had everything in it but peace up to the moment I invited the Lord into my life. Now, I was finally at peace with myself. I wasn't really sure what I had done, where I was going to go, or anything else, for that matter. All I knew was that I was at peace with myself, knowing I had made the right decision to trust Christ as my Savior."

Harry looked at Bill and said, "I know you're right. But how do I do it?" Bill simply said, "Let's pray," and while the chaplain and the inmate prayed, Harry Greene trusted Jesus as his Savior.

But now came the tough part. It was one thing to spend a few dramatic moments alone with the chaplain, isolated from the taunts and ridicule of his fellow inmates, but what would it be like when Harry returned to his cell block? What would the other inmates say and think? Aware that the spirit of God would make him a different person, Harry wisely chose not to wear his newfound faith on his sleeve.

"I was actually very quiet about my conversion when I returned to my cell and in the days following," Harry recalls. "Still, something amazing happened—and it occurred almost immediately. One of my cell mates, who later came to Christ through the same ministry, said to me, 'Hey, man, are you feeling all right? You don't seem like your old self.' Well, he was right. I wasn't like my old self. I had become a new person because of the saving grace of my new friend, Jesus Christ. I've got to admit, though, I didn't think anyone would take any notice of the 'new Harry' so quickly. What had happened, I guess, without my even realizing it, was that a new creation had already begun to take shape."

The good news is that Harry's new faith in Christ stuck. He truly had become a new creature: old things were fast passing away, and all things were becoming new—even as he sat there quietly in his cell. Harry says, "Within a matter of days, I signed up for the Bible lessons and the Bible study correspondence courses that Bill made available to us. I also began to go over to the bars and listen to the services—for the first time, really. And those Christian volunteers I couldn't stand for all those months? Well, I began to listen to them, because what they had to say unexpectedly now made sense. I even asked them questions about the Bible and the Christian faith. I couldn't get enough of their fellowship."

> **"My precious grandmother, the lady who had prayed for me every day of my life, finally saw her prayers answered. And to think I had always told her she was wasting her time."**

But Harry had a problem. While his greatest desire was to go into depth in understanding God's Word and the Christian faith, he realized that he didn't own a Bible. For that, however, he knew there would be one easy remedy. "I wrote my grandmother right away and asked her to send me a study Bible," he says. "I can still remember the day it arrived. My precious grandmother, the lady who had prayed so fervently for me every day of my life, finally saw her prayers answered. Early on, she knew my 'conversion' at camp—when I walked forward to please her—had been fakery of the highest order. There was no fooling her, and down deep I knew she knew it. Her response, however, to my lack of spiritual sincerity was never to judge me, but simply to keep praying for her wayward grandson. Now, the prodigal had seen the many errors of his ways and had requested a Bible—a book I literally wore out over the next two years."

Chaplain Bill Simmer was eager to nurture Harry's new faith, and he arranged for him to meet Sheriff J. Elwood Clements. In the months to come, Bill would often appeal to the sheriff to give Harry privileges to help him with his growing responsibilities and in his faith. But first, Bill wisely felt there was a need for reconciliation between Harry and his family. So he arranged for a Sunday morning visit.

The Sunday arrived, and Harry waited anxiously in a small visitation room, afraid and ashamed of what his parents might say. When his mother and father entered the room, Harry did his best to keep things under control, but his mother began crying. "How could you do this to us?" she moaned. "Don't you know what we've been through? What did we do wrong? You don't belong here, Harry," his mother said, tears streaming down her cheeks. Harry's dad didn't say much, but he did say he would stand by his son, which greatly surprised Harry given the challenges of their past relationship. It was only a thirty-minute meeting, and Harry did everything possible to maintain his composure. But inside he was destroyed, so he told his parents never to come visit him again in jail. It was just too hard for him.

After his folks had left the room, Harry stood there motionless. The usual affable smile had departed. His lack of sensitivity had inflicted mountains of pain on his family, and his thoughtlessness had made today's family reunion one of regret. Suddenly, the brief reverie was punctuated by the slam of a metal door, and Harry returned to Cell Block C. In jail or prison, inmates dare not show their sensitive side since it's considered an act of weakness. So Harry stayed tough on the outside. Only he knew the turmoil that churned within. After the evening count he buried his face deeply into the pillow and sobbed quietly. It was one of the worst days of his life.

> **"I remember saying to myself, This is it; this is my last day in jail. God is going to deliver me from these iron bars, and I'm going to be free because I'm a Christian."**

Harry's faith was becoming stronger with each passing day. God's Word had become as vital as physical food, and the Holy Spirit was living demonstrably in his life. Harry felt so good about how things were going, in fact, that during those weeks as a new Christian, he had fully persuaded himself that when the court date arrived, the judge would be thrilled with his conversion, see the dramatic changes in his life, forgive Harry for his numerous transgressions, and put the machinery in motion that would soon set the young inmate free. Harry recalls, "I remember saying to myself, *This is it; this is my last day in jail. God is going to deliver me from these iron bars, and I'm going to be free because I'm a Christian.* I was convinced that day would be my last day in jail, even though I had intended to plead guilty because that's what I thought a Christian should do. My decision was confirmed after talking it over with Chaplain Bill, who said I had no choice but to plead guilty to my crimes of fraud. Bill said, 'Harry, you need to do what God lays on your heart. You'll know the right thing to do.' Well, God laid on my heart the importance of going into that courtroom and pleading guilty."

"The morning of my court date, I got up happy and confident that I'd soon be a free man. When I had arrived in my cell block months earlier, the authorities had given me a toothbrush, towel, and a few personal items—all of which I now left on my bunk, figuring someone could throw them away or wash them or do whatever they wanted to do with them. I knew I wouldn't need them any longer, because I wasn't going to be back.

"Well, the moment finally came for me to have my day in court. My lawyer told me, 'Harry, I know the Commonwealth Attorney is going to recommend five years, but I'm sure that's not going to happen.'

"So I'm thinking, *Fine. Fantastic. I'm going to be free. Hey, the man can recommend fifty years if he wants to. It won't matter, because I'll never serve the time. God will deliver me.* Well, sure enough, the Commonwealth Attorney said the state recommended a five-year sentence for Harry Greene."

Harry was dressed in a suit, and his lawyer, twice his age, patted him on the shoulder, assuring him that all would go well. Harry knew he easily deserved a sentence of as much as fifty years. Now, standing before the judge, he expressed his deep remorse for his crimes and told the judge he had benefited from his time served. Harry knew according to the Scripture that he was a new creature in Christ, and therefore had no doubt he would walk out of Cell Block C a free man that night.

The black-robed judge was formal and proper. The prosecution recommended five years, which was expected. So far, so good. But the butterflies were still getting into formation inside Harry's stomach. He knew the judge had the power of clemency and could immediately put into effect an exercise of mercy—which was precisely what Harry expected.

The judge then looked down at the young inmate and said in a commanding voice, "I sentence you to two years in the state penitentiary in Richmond."

You don't understand! Harry screamed in his mind, so stunned he couldn't speak.

The judge then looked down at the young inmate and said in a commanding voice, "I sentence you to two years in the state penitentiary in Richmond."

The court was quiet. Still in shock, Harry was brought to a side room, as if he were in a trance, where he changed from his suit back into his jail uniform. So much for freedom. Harry was still in jail—except now, it would only get worse.

Harry will tell you today there is no way he could ever express how he felt at that moment. "I don't have words strong enough to describe my disappointment and my total lack of belief in what I had just heard," he says. "If you've ever been in front of a judge, you know what I mean: the person sitting up there in that black robe has the power to do with your life whatever he or she wills, and there is nothing you can do about it, absolutely nothing. Not only did I feel helpless, lost, and chagrined, but I also felt anger—in fact, such rage shot through my body that I wanted to scream. I felt like saying, *Look, Judge, you just can't do this to me. I'm a Christian! God has changed me. Look at me. I'm not that bad person I once was. Give me a break. Please, Judge, give me a chance. I promise I'll prove myself.* But my mouth wouldn't open. It wasn't that I didn't know what I wanted to say; I literally could not speak. A moment or two after the sentence, they turned me around, and my lawyer said, 'I'll talk to you later,' and I went back to jail."

Harry returned to Cell Block C—to the bunk where his toothbrush and neatly folded towel remained, just as he'd left them. Sitting on the side of his bunk, Harry, in his spiritual immaturity, complained to himself, "Where the hell is God now?" Suddenly the fire of the Holy Spirit that had so captured his life was quenched. Doubting God's existence—and questioning any personal regard the Almighty might have for his jailed child—Harry went into a funk as he put everything he had learned about God, salvation, and being a new creature on hold, considering the past months as a "jailhouse Christian" as so much game playing.

> **"For the life of me I couldn't tell you what he prayed about, but I'm sure it was something like, 'God, right now, give Harry peace and strength.'"**
> **Once again, God was true to His word. He answered Bill's prayer.**

Chaplain Bill knew how Harry was feeling, so he came to the dejected prisoner's cell block and took Harry aside. Harry remembers, "That was the day I think I finally learned the true value of prayer. There I was, back in jail, when I had felt absolute confidence that I would be set free. So what could Bill possibly want to pray about? Would he continue the charade? Pretend that God was still alive in His heavens and that He really cared about me? Well, it was no charade at all. Bill just started to pray in the quietness of that moment. For the life of me I cannot tell you what he prayed about, but I'm sure it was something like, 'God, right now, give

Harry peace and strength.'" Once again, God was true to His word. He answered Bill's prayer.

During that time of prayer, Harry again learned what it meant to enjoy a peace that passes all understanding, because when Bill had finished praying, Harry knew he truly accepted what had happened to him earlier that day in court. Harry says, "I know some people might say, 'Well, of course you accepted it. What choice did you have? You were in jail, and now you were going to prison.' To that I'd simply say this: you can accept something for one of two reasons. One, because there is no alternative, or two, because you believe God has a divine plan for your life—regardless of the obstacles placed before you. When Bill finished praying, I didn't know what was going to happen to me, but I had an inner peace that said, *Okay, I know where God is . . . He's still in my heart.* That's when I knew where I needed to be—in God's Word, and trusting Him as I'd never trusted Him before."

Good News chaplains are always straightforward with inmates, helping them understand that making a choice to accept Christ does not eliminate the consequences of their bad choices that landed them in jail. The chaplain is quick to remind inmates that the jail doors will not necessarily swing open, setting the prisoner free. However, chaplains do tell inmates about the choice they have to accept Christ—a choice that will give them a kind of freedom they never experienced in this world. There is a saying in prison: "If you can't do the time, don't do the crime." Unfortunately, many prisoners hear this counsel too late."

Now, Harry was bracing himself for prison, a place he'd heard all about. "During those painful moments of awareness, Bill remained at my side—always showing up at the right time: loving, kind, helpful, nonjudgmental," Harry says. "He had become my pastor, mentor, and friend. Bill was valuable to me not just because he'd directed me to the Person of Jesus

Christ, but because he was always there when I needed a friend most. Good News Chaplain Dan Matsche, Regional Director for Good News Jail & Prison Ministry in Colorado, said something years ago that continues to ring true in my life and ministry today: 'The chaplaincy is a hands-on pastoral ministry of presence.' And that's how God used Bill to help me get through that day. Now that I was finally able to accept the judge's decision, I returned to my cell and started reading the Scriptures again, doing the Bible studies, and looking down what I knew would still be a long, winding road—but more than willing to trust God to show me His way."

> **"This assignment was really exciting for me, not only because I was granted a little more freedom, but also because I got to look at a different tree every day—not the same one I'd seen day after day from my cell window for the past four months."**

If anyone ever questions whether God can change a life, it would be wise for that person to spend a few hours with ex-con Harry L. Greene. In fact, the change in Harry's attitude was so dramatic that they made him a jail trustee. With that special privilege, Harry was able to get out of his cell block every day to assume the lowly job of janitor. Lowly or not, however, Harry remembers with joy, "This assignment was exciting for me, not only because I was granted a little more freedom, but also because I got to look at a different tree every day—not the same one I'd seen day after day from my cell window for the past four months. Until you've gazed at the same tree limb for months on end and seen it go through its cycles, it's hard to realize what real confinement is. Now, as a jail trustee, I was feeling better. Suddenly, I had real work to do. I know that God intervened for me in this situation because normally, the only way to get out of that cell block would be if your time were up, you went to court, or if you had a visitor. And I didn't have any visitors."

But there *was* one guy who wanted to get close to Harry—close enough, in fact, to kill him. The inmate in question was in for murder, so he probably figured, *What's the big deal in taking another life? And why not Harry's?* The man felt that Harry had become the chaplain's "favorite" and was so angry that he determined to do something about it. Harry describes the day of the attempted assault: "As part of my janitorial duties, I would hand the inmates a mop and a broom through the bars, which they would then use to sweep their trash out into the hall and mop their floor. I would go from cell block to cell block, and then come back to where I'd started. They would then give me the stuff back, and I would go to the next cell block, pushing my broom and mop in a bucket along the floor. That was my job as trustee.

"One day, after I had put a broom and mop into a cell block and gone on to the next one, an inmate who didn't like me very much took the broom I'd given him to clean his cell and broke it across his knee. As I came back around the corner, cell block on the right, wall on the left, he took the piece with the sharp end and tried to stab me through the bars. I jumped back against the wall, just far enough out of his reach. Every time I'd move down the wall, he would also move down the bars inside his cell block. Four or five times he tried to spear me. It was touch and go, when finally I backed away to where I was out of his reach. One of the COs saw what was happening, ran over to the cell block, and removed the homemade weapon from the man. From then on, I paid special attention to this guy, because his hatred of me was unabated. He would cuss me out and carry on every time I approached his cell block." No question about it: Jesus was Harry's protector, but he still had to watch his back.

"Prison is one of the easiest places in the world to be a Christian because when you're behind bars, your focus can be totally on God. That's because you do not have to worry about making a living or supporting a family, or dealing with the things that made up your lifestyle on the outside."

It may sound strange, but you'll hear it often from believers who have been behind bars: The easiest place to be a Christian is in prison. Harry explains why this is true. "Prison is one of the easiest places in the world to be a Christian because when you're behind bars, your focus can be totally on God. That's because you do not have to worry about making a living or supporting a family, or dealing with the things that made up your lifestyle on the outside. In a way, for me, it became the ultimate mountaintop experience. As a Christian, I was happy, content, had accepted my punishment, and was convinced that everything was going to be all right. Even through the worst times, which were the holidays, I was somehow able to cope. But it wasn't easy. Thanksgiving and Christmas were the toughest because they'd always been such special times with my family. Christmas was especially difficult for me, sitting quietly there in my cell on Christmas Day. However, I'll never forget when I heard some carols echoing down the hall. I remember thinking, 'What in the world is this?' It turned out that Chaplain Bill had gone to one of the churches and invited several choir members to come and sing Christmas carols to us inmates.

But Chaplain Bill didn't stop there. He also went to a few other churches and asked people to bake chocolate chip cookies—delicacies that were wrapped in colorful napkins with beautiful red ribbons tied around them. "It was unbelievable," Harry remembers. "Carolers sang the songs of Christmas *outside our cell block*, and every inmate was given a bag of four chocolate chip cookies! It was the greatest Christmas gift I ever received—and something I will never forget as long as I live. It's those incredible little acts of kindness that make the greatest difference—not only to an inmate, but to people in every walk of life. It was only four chocolate chip cookies, but it was a moment of inexpressible joy in the middle of solitude and pain."

Looking through the long lens of time, Harry confirms that most of the challenges he faced in jail were also the source of most of his blessings. He actually wonders if he would ever have come to faith in Christ had he not been placed behind bars. He says, "When I look back on my time in jail, I realize first of all that being there was my choice; and second, that God, in His infinite wisdom, was preparing me for what I am doing today. It's a matter of biblical record that Moses, the great leader of the Children of Israel, wandered aimlessly in the wilderness for forty years; my desert ordeal— much shorter than I deserved—was serving time in jail and prison. But it was behind bars that I found my Savior.

"I can also now say in all honesty that I was blessed by God's infinite mercy that evening the police pulled my rented black Cadillac to the side of road and said, 'Mr. Greene, it's over.' I didn't understand God's reasoning at the time, but I do now. In that moment, I easily might have taken the life of a policeman—if the gun had been in my possession. Thank God it was not."

Now, it was up to Harry to come to an understanding of what God had in mind for him to do as he prepared to go to prison. Was this, too, going to be a blessing in disguise? Would he be able to stand firm in his Christian faith? What good could possibly come from a two-year prison sentence? Harry had no idea, but before long, he knew he would have at least some of the answers.

Does the presence of a Good News chaplain make a difference in the life of a man or woman behind bars? The results shown here should answer that question with finality. Because of the support and friendship of so many Christians throughout the nation, lives of people in our jails and prisons are being changed—for eternity.

GOOD NEWS JAIL & PRISON MINISTRY

MINISTRY STATISTICS
As of December 31, 2000

CATEGORY	1987-1994	1995	1996	1997	1998	1999	2000	TOTAL
Decisions For Christ	204,775	18,229	22,861	32,064	40,790	52,843	**68,716**	440,278
Preaching Services	77,276	9,693	10,536	14,773	15,126	15,720	**21,584**	164,708
Bible Classes	134,993	18,606	22,256	28,005	34,660	40,429	**50,126**	329,075
Individual Counseling Sessions	590,213	55,649	57,230	76,466	80,918	86,327	**121,669**	1,068,472
Bible Lessons Completed	1,992,785	200,736	211,857	264,090	278,500	327,159	**338,019**	3,613,146

Harry Greene, 6 years old   Harry Greene, High School Senior

Harry Greene, High School Graduation – 1961

Harry Greene, U.S. Army – 1962

Harry Greene,
Virginia State
Penitentiary –
1965

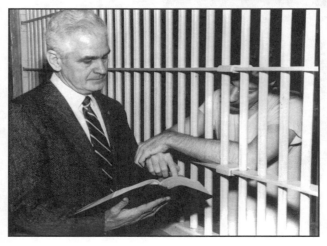

Founder/ Chaplain
Dr. William L. (Bill)
Simmer

Harry Greene, far left, in ministry Halfway House after release – 1966

Sheriff J. Elwood Clements, left, Harry and Chaplain Bill Simmer

Copy of pardon from Governor of Virginia

COMMONWEALTH OF VIRGINIA

EXECUTIVE DEPARTMENT

To All to Whom These Presents Shall Come—Greeting:

Whereas, *at a* Circuit, Circuit, Corporation, respectively, *Court held in and for the* County, County, City, respectively, *of* Arlington, Fairfax, Alexandria, respectively, *in the month of* Jan., April & Oct., Oct. & Nov., respectively, *in the year one thousand nine hundred and* sixty-five, sixty-five, sixty-five, respectively,

HARRY LYNN GREENE, a/k/a RICHARD WAYNE GEARY, a/k/a HARRY ADAMS

was convicted of grand larceny - 2 counts, grand larceny - 2 counts, worthless checks, respectively, *and was thereupon sentenced to* total term - 2 years.

and whereas it appears to the Executive that relying on the recommendations of reputable citizens who are familiar with this man's conduct since his release,

that he *is a fit subject for clemency:*

Therefore, I, Linwood Holton , *Governor of the Commonwealth of Virginia, have, by virtue of authority vested in me, pardoned and do hereby pardon the said*

HARRY LYNN GREENE, a/k/a RICHARD WAYNE GEARY, a/k/a HARRY ADAMS

Given under my hand and under the Letter Seal of the Commonwealth at Richmond, this 12th *day of* October , *in the year of our Lord one thousand nine hundred and* seventy-two *and in the* 197th *year of the Commonwealth.*

Governor of Virginia.

By the Governor:

Secretary of the Commonwealth.

Harry, Barbara,
Matthew & Sara –
1978

Copy of appointment to
Virginia State Board of
Corrections by Governor
Charles Robb – 1982

COMMONWEALTH
of
VIRGINIA

TO ALL TO WHOM THESE PRESENTS SHALL COME - GREETING

Know Ye *that from special trust and confidence reposed in his fidelity, our Governor by virtue of authority vested in him by law, hath appointed and hereby commissions*

HARRY LYNN GREENE

a member of the State Board of Corrections, effective July 1, 1982, to serve for a term of four years, ending June 30, 1986, subject to confirmation by the General Assembly.

In Testimony Whereof *our said Governor hath hereunto signed his name and affixed the Lesser Seal of the Commonwealth at Richmond this* thirtieth *day of* June *in the year of our Lord, one thousand nine hundred* eighty-two *and in the* two-hundred seventh *year of the Commonwealth*

Charles S. Robb
Governor

Secretary of the Commonwealth

Harry and brother,
Dennis – 1991

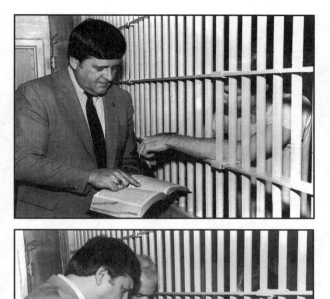

Harry, after becoming President of Good News, ministering in jail – 1983

Harry and President Emeritus Bill Simmer ministering together – 1983

Harry's licensing to the ministry of the Gospel by Barcroft Bible Church – May 20, 1984

Certificate of Licensing

This is to certify that **Barcroft Bible Church** , after a careful examination by the Board of Elders concerning Christian testimony, call to the ministry, and the doctrinal statement of this assembly, as well as a careful investigation in regard to the possession of spiritual gifts, solemnly and publicly set apart and licensed

Harry L. Greene

to the work of **The Ministry of the Gospel** of Jesus Christ in the name of the Father, the Son, and the Holy Spirit, on the ___20th___ day of the month of ___May___ ₁₉84

_____   _____
Moderator   Clerk

The Board of Elders:

Harry receiving the Billy
Graham Insitute for Prison
Ministries Annual Award from
Director Don Smarto in 1991

Harry awarded a Doctor
of Humanities degree
from International
Graduate School in
Honolulu, Hawaii – 1992

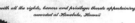

International Graduate School

Honolulu, Hawaii

Upon recommendation of the Faculty and by virtue of the Authority
vested in the Board of Regents
hereby confers upon

Harry L. Greene

the degree of

Doctor of Humanities

with all the rights, honors and privileges thereto appertaining
awarded at Honolulu, Hawaii

May 17, 1992

Good News
Headquarters
Building in
Richmond,
Virginia – 1995

Good News Headquarters
Building in Richmond,
Virginia – 1995

Harry and Barabra's
wedding with
Harry's parents, Bill
& Maggie Mae
Greene – 1966

Harry's Grandmother –
Kitty Sullivan

Good News Founders –
Dr. William and Helen Simmer

Harry & Barbara

Harry, Barbara,
Matthew and Sara

Chapter 7

If You Think Jail's Bad, Wait 'til You Get to Prison!

If you can't do the time, don't do the crime.

ituated high on a hill in the old part of the city, the Virginia State Penitentiary, now demolished, was located at 500 Spring Street in Richmond. Dating back to 1797, the facility was commissioned by Thomas Jefferson. Its original cells were built in a circular pattern designed to provide solitary confinement for each prisoner. This innovative approach provided the maximum number of cells for viewing by a CO located in the center of the circle.

In his wildest dreams, Harry never figured such an historic institution would be his home. Jail was bad enough; now he could look forward to yet another nightmare. The toughest part for Harry was waiting in Cell Block C in anticipation of that fateful day when he would get the word that it was time to make the move to his new quarters. "You never knew when you were going to be sent to prison once you'd been assigned," Harry explains. "It all depended on when they wanted to pick you up—something they did when they were good and ready. I saw it happen on several occasions with my fellow inmates: *now you see them, now you don't.* When the time came to haul someone away, the COs would come barging into the cell block, yell at the prisoner to grab his things, and make their exit. Suddenly, you're on your way to prison—simple as that. No fanfare. No brass bands. You just grab your things and go . . . and that's what happened to me when they came to get me on a morning I will never forget."

Carrying with him only a few earthly possessions, Harry was chained and handcuffed in preparation for the journey to Richmond. He would not be alone that day, however, for outside the jail a large group of prisoners had already been assembled from other institutions in the area, inmates who would be his traveling companions on the bus that would take them to the next phase of their punishment, about one hundred miles away.

"As soon as I entered my cage, I quickly counted twenty prisoners cramped together. Before I got out and was transferred to a cell, there were thirty of us."

It was a cold, rainy day in the autumn of the year—a dismal physical setting that mirrored the despair Harry was feeling as the bus, crowded with prisoners, bumped its way along toward its final destination. It was not easy to see the prison at first, but Harry remembers squinting at what appeared to be an old gothic structure, a fortress with ancient walls and turrets, like a wide shot of the castle from the movie *Frankenstein*. The bus, inching slowly through the foggy darkness, finally pulled to a stop in front of the prison at around 7 P.M. Harry says, "It was the scariest and most eerie thing I had ever seen. Because I'd heard so many stories about prison life and had talked to scores of inmates who had been in and out of prison so often, I thought I would be ready for what I was about to experience. Not so. Hearing about prison and arriving at its formidable doors as a chained, handcuffed prisoner are two entirely different things. One is theory; the other, reality. That day was reality for me. I was aware that some of the guys I knew from Cell Block C were in there, so if I was lucky, I thought I might eventually see them, hoping they would show me the ropes. I figured I'd need all the help I could get."

The first items of business for Harry were getting booked into the facility, receiving a prison number, and then posing for the traditional mug shot: one straight on, one side view. Harry stood patiently in line and did what he was told. He recalls, "In those days in Virginia, the authorities would take the inmates to what they called a holding area, where they would keep prisoners for anywhere from two weeks to thirty days prior to assigning them to their cells. These were not elegant accommodations; instead, we were hustled into fortified wire cages that had been built and placed in a large room—chain link on all sides and across the top, with a door in the side for entry. As I entered my new quarters, I looked around and counted six of these large cages, positioned in a square, all facing each other. In the center of the cages was a small table where two COs sat. As I entered my cage, I counted twenty prisoners cramped together. Before I got out and was later transferred to my cell, there were thirty of us. Tight quarters, especially when there was no one I wanted to be with—either inside or out of prison!"

Harry grabbed one of the bunk beds—more like Army cots—and tried to make himself at home, sitting there with only the clothes on his back, since he was allowed no personal belongings whatsoever. After about ten minutes, the COs ordered everyone who'd just arrived on the bus to get out of the cage and strip themselves naked. "We were taken to the showers, after which we received a cold vinegar bath, a delousing procedure which was very unpleasant, especially if a prisoner had open cuts or sores," Harry remembers. "But lice had to be destroyed, and the prison authorities apparently figured they had perfected the art of killing the little creatures.

After this humiliating experience, which concluded with a not-so-thrilling body cavity examination, we were handed our blue denim prison uniforms and taken back to our cages. Welcome to prison—day one!"

The area where Harry and the other prisoners sat in their cages was as bright as a high school football stadium on game night, with immense lights overhead that shone their brilliance on them day and night. Not once were the lights turned off. There the inmates sat, wondering what would happen to them next, while all the time the two COs sat at their little table going about their business, ignoring the agitated, caged prisoners and whatever needs they might have. Harry recalls, "I had no idea what to expect that first night in prison, but it was not long before I found out, because I suddenly began to hear the terrified cries of a man in the cage next to mine as he was being raped repeatedly—my guess was at least ten times—by his fellow inmates. One by one, the prisoners in his cage had their brutal way with him. To this day I have not heard such screaming. His cries lasted for the better part of an hour, and the mournful sounds of his ordeal still echo in my head.

"One by one, the prisoners in his cage had their brutal way with him. To this day I have not heard such screaming."

"And it all happened within a few feet of where the two COs sat; yet not once did they turn their heads in the direction of the man's screams or attempt to do anything about it. The more he screamed, the more I thought, *You may try that with me guys, but you're going to have to kill me to do it.* I've never been so scared. And that was only the first night! I wish I could say that things improved in the days following. They did not."

About a week later, as Harry and his fellow inmates were being marched to breakfast down at the chow hall, an inmate from a line marching on the other side reached up to the prisoner in front of him and slit his throat from ear to ear with a homemade blade. His head just flopped back, decapitated. The dead body dropped to the ground, and the other prisoners kept marching. No one looked . . . no one stopped . . . and no one said a word. Harry recalls thinking, *What am I into here?* "I never found out if the killer was charged for the murder, nor did I ever ask," he says. "You don't ask those kinds of questions in prison. There's enough of your own stuff to attend to. You don't mess with the business of others.

"But the more violence I saw, the more sense it made to me to pray each day for my physical and spiritual protection. Prison is a demonic place, and I saw things behind those walls that clearly illustrated the concept of man's inhumanity to his fellow man. In that perverted environment, inmates with strong sexual desires preyed mightily on the weak. On more than one occasion I wished I'd gone to Vietnam. *It couldn't have been this bad!* Wherever I looked I could see the penitentiary was fertile ground for Satan, but I had chosen to follow the Savior and had made the decision not to turn away from my commitment to the Lord and His Word."

> ## "The unwritten rule among COs is simply, as long as you're not killing one another or doing something terribly bad, then we'll leave you alone."

It's tough enough in the outside world to know whom you can trust when push comes to shove; multiply that suspicion by a thousand, and that's about how much a prisoner feels he can trust his fellow inmates. That's because the prisoners, to a large degree, run the prisons. Harry explains, "People always ask me why this is the case. Aren't the COs in charge? Don't they lay down the law to the prisoners and expect them to comply? Well, yes and no. A CO has no weapon other than perhaps a baton and some mace. He knows if the prisoners riot, they're going to take him down. No question about that. That's why whenever there's a prison riot, you always read about the COs being captured and held hostage: *they have no defense.* If you're a CO up on the wall—in one of the gun turrets—then you're armed, but not within the prison itself. So, the unwritten rule among COs is simply, as long as you're not killing one another or doing something terribly bad, then we'll leave you alone. I always wondered what the meaning of 'bad' was for them. It certainly was a definition different from my own."

Harry remained in his cage for two weeks before he was assigned to his cell: prisoner Harry L. Greene, number 87349, a convicted felon, losing all rights for owning property, voting, being bonded, and numerous other civil rights, all which he forfeited under that condition. Harry says, "It was a relief finally to be released from my cage and all it represented and sent to a cell. It turned out that I was the cell mate of a prisoner I had met earlier in jail where we had become friends—that is, if a person can really have a friend in jail. His name was Bruce, a kind of guardian angel to me for the first couple of days when I was out in the actual prison yard. Bruce told me when to watch my back and whom to avoid. His counsel saved the day for me on more than one occasion, because when you're a new guy in prison, invariably old timers will come up to you and offer you a cigarette, some candy, or whatever they can give you to put you in their debt. *But once you get into their debt, they've got you in their pocket.*"

Harry soon learned the reality of that statement, as he observed that much of the brutality in prison—inmates getting stabbed, raped, and beaten—often took place because someone failed to repay a debt—further compounded by the human hatred, homosexuality, and ethnic bigotry that always reigned supreme. "There are cliques inside those walls, and every prison has them," Harry says. "Some are racially or religiously motivated; others come together through specific interests. For example, if I like country and western music and enjoy that lifestyle, then I'm going to gravitate towards those in prison who are of like mind. If I like rock 'n roll or if I enjoy rap music, it will be the same thing. Prisoners, if they're smart, learn this quickly—so they can know whom to trust within the group. But even then, no one can ever be sure he'll be 100 percent safe. You just try to get into a group that isn't in confrontation or combat with another clique. But if conflict does occur, you need to be ready to defend yourself. I was fortunate that I was six-foot, three inches and two hundred-plus pounds, and looked as if I could take care of myself. Some might say that's why no one picked on me. But it was more than my size. God protected me. That's all I can really say: *God protected me*."

> ## "I was fortunate that I was six-foot, three inches, two hundred-plus pounds, and looked as if I could take care of myself."

If prison is the graduate school of crime, it must also be considered a twenty-four-hour classroom for observing human life in all its gross, godless depravity. Harry's memories of the decadence of prison life remain fresh in his mind: "I saw homosexual acts from my cell that were so cruel and violent it was just unreal. It turned my stomach, but I didn't dare say or

do anything. I had quickly learned the rules of non-involve-
ment. It was the same with drugs. The delivery and use of nar-
cotics were equally prevalent as I saw controlled substances
permeate the prison. Over the years, people have often asked
me, 'How can drugs possibly make their way into an institution?' Well, there's only one way: *someone has to bring them
in*. They don't grow there, normally. When I was in prison, the
COs were barely making a living wage. So if I'm a prisoner I
say to a CO, 'Look, how'd you like to pick up an extra couple
hundred bucks? All you have to do is bring some drugs in for
me, and I'll take care of you.' Or a prisoner might say to the
CO, 'Hey, how'd you like to spend a weekend of wild, nonstop
sex with my girlfriend or my wife? That should be enough
payment for the drugs.' This was probably one of the most
effective ploys used by prisoners against the COs, because
once they developed this 'business' relationship, the prisoner
figured, *Ha, I've got you*. And once COs were 'gotten,' they
had to continue to cooperate in their illegal schemes or suffer the consequences of being turned in by the prisoner. It
had all the possibilities of becoming a never-ending cycle.
And something else: if you're a CO and I'm a CO, you're not
going to tell me that you're in trouble with the inmates. That's
one more 'gotcha.'"

It didn't take long for Harry to see how creative his fellow inmates could be on many fronts, particularly in their ability to make their own booze—by allowing accumulated raisins
and pieces of fruit to ferment in the cell toilet. Not a very
appetizing procedure, perhaps, but the hooch was drinkable
and always seemed to provide the buzz prisoners were looking for. Another innovative method of producing cell-made
brew was to strain a few spoonfuls of shaving lotion through
pieces of white bread and drink it. Harry recalls, "Now that's a
combination that would put you on your can fast, because it
was just pure alcohol."

What makes Harry's story particularly fascinating—and the stories of all prisoners intriguing—is that all this institutional activity takes place in the context of the misguided belief that we are actually *rehabilitating* the prisoner. For more than two hundred years, society has spent billions of dollars trying to rehabilitate people by putting them behind bars with *people just like themselves*. However, the definition of *rehabilitate* reads "to restore to its former condition or state." Harry stresses we are doing just that.

> **For more than two hundred years, society has spent billions of dollars trying to rehabilitate people by putting them behind bars with people just like themselves.**

"We are indeed 'rehabilitating' prisoners, because we are taking criminals of varying degrees into our institutions, where they learn to become better at their evil crafts, and then turning them out as even more effective enemies of society," he says. "That's why prison must be seen as *the graduate school of crime*. For this reason, the rate of recidivism will always be high. I speak from firsthand knowledge, because I know I could have learned how to commit virtually any criminal act imaginable while I was in that prison: physical crimes, boosting a car, assault, armed robbery, embezzlement, forgery, cracking safes. My would-be tutors were everywhere within those walls—and they were ready to teach. An education was in progress in that environment that wasn't being paid for by the state, but which the state was *de facto* endorsing because it was implying that *we're going to put you all together and we're going to teach you how to be good guys*. Nonsense. No one is going to teach anyone how to be a good guy unless he or she wants to change.

Full Pardon

"Intelligent people have insisted, *Change the behavior and the person will change,* so, believing this, we've allocated hundreds of millions of dollars for good—and needed—educational, vocational, and psychological programs for prisoners. But God says, *No, you've got it backwards. Change the person, and the behavior will change.* And, that's the essence of Good News Jail & Prison Ministry. Our chaplains are taking the Gospel of Jesus Christ, the only power on earth that can change a heart, so that with God's help a man or woman can discover the resources to change from the inside out.

"That's what happened to me in that confinement cell with Chaplain Bill. I was changed forever by the refreshing, liberating Gospel of Jesus Christ. The good news for me was that when I left that jail, God did not stay there in Cell Block C while I went to prison in Richmond. *God went to prison with me.* If He had not, I don't even want to consider what might have happened to me. Had Christ not changed my belligerent, cocky, and combative attitude, someone would have probably killed me—and I probably would have deserved it."

But Harry survived his prison ordeal. Why? "Because a loving God went with me to Richmond, to that gothic fortress on the hill, where He continued to give me peace, patience, and a perseverance that saw me through some of the darkest days of my life," Harry says. "And it all happened because *every day* a relentless, God-fearing chaplain kept sticking his nose into Cell Block C, preaching the Word, talking the Truth, loving inmates who'd never known real love in their lives, putting his hand on our shoulders, and trying to convince us we were worth something after all. That message in particular—*that we weren't scum, but worthy in God's sight*—is what turned many of us around. It not only won the day; it won our hearts."

Prison is hell on earth. Prisoners can never relax. They are forever on their guard, watching their backs, always wondering whom they dare trust. Life is miserable. Prisoners don't live; they exist. If they do any work, it's usually meaningless. Little of what is provided is ever resource enough for change. Of course, the prison system, if it could talk, would say, *Hey, wait a minute. That's not our job. We're here to house criminals. The corrections system is designed to separate the bad people from the rest of society so that people can feel safe. But it's not our job to change the individual.* It's reminiscent of the old story of the little boy who was asked by his mother to sit down at the table for supper. The child says, "Okay, mom, I'll sit down on the outside, *but I want you to know that inside I'm still standing up!*" The point is this: we can provide the best advice, the most advanced psychological counseling, and the most carefully researched programs available, and we still will not succeed in forcing a man or woman to do something he or she does not want to do. Not in prison; not on the outside.

Prison is hell on earth.
Prisoners can never relax.

Since most of Harry's life has been involved with people behind bars, it makes sense to hear him speak more fully on this issue, "In my opinion, there's a tremendous difference between change and benefit," he explains. "Benefits are external; change comes from the inside out. When a prisoner tells one of our Good New chaplains, 'I am going to change!' that decision does not come about from getting a GED or from signing up for a vocational program. It never has, and it never will. External programs change no one's heart. What changes the spirit of a prisoner—or anyone, for that matter—is the internal change that *manifests itself on the outside* when he or she takes advantage of those options to better himself or herself. People need to learn how to read. They need occupational skills, and they certainly need to know where their strengths and weaknesses lie to improve their lot in life. But, *those are benefits of the system* to those who want to change. In and of themselves, externals change no one.

The late Supreme Court Justice Warren Berger once said that any significant change he had ever seen in a criminal's life came from a "God base." The leadership of Good News Jail & Prison Ministry could not agree more. But until this message of hope and *real change* through a profound relationship with Jesus Christ becomes available to all of the hundreds of thousands of men and women behind bars, our institutions will simply become more violent and more treacherous, making necessary larger and larger cages to house those who are a danger to society—and who probably will become an even greater menace upon their release.

While working with prisoners is serious business, Harry is never far from using humor to help him diagnose the ills he sees in how we view our prison system today. He tells the story of some brave souls who went moose hunting in the far north:

"Two hunters loved to go to the wilds of Canada to hunt and fish. One year they traveled to a location they loved so much that they decided to return the following year. So again, as they did the year before, they hired a seaplane, since there were no roads in the area, to fly them in and land them on a lake. They made their way to shore and began their quest of Canadian moose.

"The pilot shouts to the hunters, 'I'll be back in a week, and I know you're going to go moose hunting. So remember, we can only take one moose per person out of here. Any more than that, and it will be too much weight for the plane.'

"The hunters agree and promise to be back at the designated spot in seven days. As scheduled, a week later the pilot returns, lands on the lake, coasts up to the shore where the hunters had pitched their tents, and sees a high stack of moose lying near the shore—six moose, in fact.

"The pilot goes ballistic, saying, 'There's no way in the world we can get this many moose out of here.'

"To which the hunters respond, 'Look, we've got this figured out. We tie three moose on each of the plane's two pontoons, distribute the weight evenly, and you go to the end of the lake, where you just give it as much power as you can to take off, and we'll be in good shape. We'll be just fine. That's how we did it last year. So don't worry.'

"The pilot says, 'There's no way it's going to work, and I'm not going to do it.'

"'Look,' said the hunters, 'We'll give you $500 extra if you'll do it just this one time.'

"'Well, that's different. Except I still don't know if we can do it,' the pilot says as they taxi to the end of the lake with six moose strapped on the two pontoons, the plane almost sinking from the weight of the carcasses and the passengers.

"Then, giving it all the power available, and almost pushing his foot through to the carburetor, the plane lifts off. They almost make it past the tree line—but not quite, and they crash into the trees. The hunters and the pilot extricate themselves from the crumpled fabric and metal, pushing moose, glass, and broken parts of the plane out of their way.

"One hunter looks at the other and says, 'Do you know where we are?'

"'Yeah. I think we made it about one hundred yards further than where we crashed last year.'"

Yet another working definition of insanity: *doing the same thing repeatedly, always hoping for a different result.* It doesn't work with dead moose on pontoons, and it doesn't work by expecting miracles from otherwise well-meaning prison programs. It is the power of the living God alone, as expressed through His Son, Jesus Christ, by which systemic, permanent change takes place. And that is the mission and message of the Good News chaplains—to stand in the gap, to go face-to-face with our nation's prisoners, and to declare in no uncertain terms that God *can* change their hearts, revolutionize their lives, and make them whole, always reminding them of the words of Jesus: "And ye shall know the truth, and the truth shall make you free" (John 8:32). That was the freedom Harry Greene experienced the day he gave his heart to Christ in the solitary confinement cell in the Arlington County Jail—a decision that would serve him well as he endured the horrors and indignity of his sentence in the Virginia State Penitentiary.

> **It is only the power of the living God as expressed through His Son, Jesus Christ, by which systemic, permanent change takes place.**

Once released from prison, Harry would be living proof that God truly does change people from the inside. It would not be an easy road, but he knew that with God all things are possible. Harry also knew that he would never be able to make it on his own, that he would need the years of wisdom, spiritual counsel, and friendship of the one who had brought him to Christ, his valued friend and spiritual father, Chaplain Bill Simmer—a man of God who remained at Harry's side when the young felon needed him most.

Full Pardon

While serving as a career police officer, Karl Holsberg was led by his five-year-old daughter to give his life to Jesus Christ, promising to follow wherever the Lord might lead. Soon thereafter, Karl found himself studying God's Word in Evangel Theological Seminary. After graduating with a master of divinity degree and being ordained as a Congregational minister, Karl and his wife, Robbie, served two tours as missionaries in India. After retirement from law enforcement, Karl devoted his time to a national drug and alcohol abuse ministry and local church activities. Later, a call would come from a Sheriff and the Good News Jail & Prison Ministry to consider a chaplaincy position—at the time, not a comfortable option, but one that he prayerfully considered.

Karl answered the call approximately six months later and agreed to become chaplain at the Fairfax County Adult Detention Center in Fairfax, Virginia. Under his leadership, the chaplaincy flourished, and five years later Karl was transferred to the Orange County Correction Center in Orlando, Florida, to serve as its senior chaplain. Karl now serves Good News as a Regional Director in the southeast United States, where he facilitates the ministries of numerous Good News chaplains, counting each day as a great blessing and opportunity to continue to serve the Lord Jesus Christ in the criminal justice arena. As the Lord brings Karl and his ministry to mind, we urge you to pray that he will continue to be an effective Servant Leader to the chaplains he oversees enabling them to minister more effectively to the thousands of inmates in their facilities.

Chapter 8

Prisoner of the State . . . Captive of Christ

Yet for love's sake I rather beseech thee,
being such an one as Paul the aged,
and now also a prisoner of Jesus Christ.
Philemon 1:9

arry wanted nothing more than to be released from that imposing penitentiary on the hill, but such a sentiment was easier to wish for than to bring to reality. Even though he was considered an exemplary prisoner, Harry still had time to serve for the crimes he'd committed. He could think thoughts of freedom all he wanted, but when he woke up in the morning, he found himself still locked in an ancient fortress, and still without any immediate hope of receiving his cherished freedom. Harry's routine had now become a waiting game, and the young convicted felon, wearing prison number 87349, remembers it well.

"The penitentiary had a large yard with a ball field where we had fierce competition in all kinds of athletic contests," Harry says. "Imagine playing football, basketball, softball—or even horseshoes—with a bunch of convicts who were always cursing, yelling, shoving, and kicking whenever the opportunity presented itself, and I think you'll get the picture. To make matters worse, there was no umpire or referee to call any of the games for fairness or lack of it, nor did any arbiters ever appear on the sidelines to step in and control the hitting. More than once I saw guys playing softball who'd just take the bat and hit a guy over the head with it. I mean, just open up his skull. We just went out there and did our thing—probably

111

as much to rid ourselves of pent-up frustrations as anything. But anything was better than being locked up inside that cell, even if we did get a bit roughed up in the process. I supposed you could call our games in the yard organized chaos."

"If I'd murdered someone during our planned armed robbery, that electric chair could easily have been my destination."

Whether they were in the yard playing ball, sitting in their cells, working in the laundry, making license plates, or eating in the mess hall, one thing was always lodged somewhere in the prisoners' minds: the Virginia State Penitentiary had a death row and an electric chair, and whether or not an inmate was headed for it, everyone knew it played an active role in the life of the prison. Harry says, "On more than one occasion, I realized if I had killed a policeman the day I was picked up, or if I'd murdered someone during our planned armed robbery, that electric chair could easily have been my destination. That's why I continued—and continue—to thank God for saving my life and for giving me an eternal future through the love and redemption of His Son, Jesus Christ. My growing faith in Him made my time in prison endurable."

The longer Harry was in prison, the more things he found to do. If he hadn't kept his head and body busy he might have gone crazy. That's why he spent as many hours in the yard as possible—a privilege offered to inmates as long as they did not pose a problem to the rest of the prison population. The fresh air alone would make his day, and he would fill his lungs with it whenever he could. While inside the fortress, he would take advantage of whatever work opportunities—vocational training of sorts—were available, tasks that allowed him to earn some money, the total of which would often accumulate to the astronomical amount of five to twelve cents a day. If he were lucky, sometimes he could earn *an entire quarter* for a full week's work. Harry says, "Even receiving those few cents a day gave me a sense that I was being productive as I joined the other inmates in making everything from shoes to furniture to license plates. I felt a certain level of accomplishment for my work. If inmates were making a chair, they could actually see a chair take shape. Their most insignificant achievement quickly became a personal triumph. But it wasn't all woodshop and achievement—at least not for most inmates. That's because prison, compared to jail, also provided a greater opportunity to get into trouble. Jail is where everyone goes who's arrested; you have to be convicted to go to prison as a felon—which makes it a much more dangerous place."

Harry recalls that in prison, inmates were clever enough to make lethal weapons out of virtually anything and everything—as prisoners continue to do today. "If you wanted to hurt someone, you just took a tooth brush, rubbed it long enough on a concrete floor, and it became a stiletto," he says. "Then, you simply wrapped some wet toilet paper around it, let it dry, and voila, you had a kind of papier-mâché handle that completed the process of producing a formidable weapon. Or you found a piece of metal—say, a nail—and you stuck it in a bar of soap so that the soap became the handle. Inmates can make a weapon out of anything. The simplest weapon, however, was to put a bar of soap in a sock—suddenly a lethal weapon—which allowed even the smallest 'David' to bring down the meanest 'Goliath' with one wild swing. Prisoners have a tremendous amount of time on their hands, so they learn to become devilishly creative, which compounds the danger to themselves and the rest of the population. That's why we always had to watch our backs."

Because there is relative autonomy of movement in prison—certainly more freedom than sitting in a county jail—there is also a greater and more open proliferation of drug deals and homosexual relationships, all of which create opportunities for inmates to end up in other's debt—something you don't want to do in prison. The very size of a prison vs. the size of the normal jail also makes prisons more lethal: there may be only fifty to four hundred people in a jail, while a prison may house as many as 2,500 or more. More inmates, more potential trouble—and more danger.

"Inmates can make a weapon out of anything."

Harry remembers how easy it was for prisoners to retaliate against one another. "Because you can't watch your back *all* the time, sooner or later you may be hurt badly," he says. "If you're a big guy, and I'm a fairly good-sized man, you'd usually be all right. But it was the little guys the inmates had to worry about. You offend a small man and he'll say to you directly—or under his breath—'You just wait, I'm gonna get you. It might be next week, next month, or six months from now, but I'll get you.' And then, when you least expect it—and usually long after you've forgotten his threat—guess what? *He gets you! Why? Because he has time to get you.* He may be looking at being locked up for ten years, but if you only have a sentence of four to five, he figures, *Hey, I don't have to do this today. I'll just let it drag on, but I will do the deed ... someday!* Grudges are huge in prison. Prisoners learn that reality from day one."

Harry was fortunate to have learned another, different reality—that he, too, was deeply indebted to One who had done so much for him. While there was no question about his

being a prisoner of the state, he had also become a prisoner—
a bond slave, as the apostle Paul called himself—to the Person
of Jesus Christ. That meant Harry had an eternal future and
that, upon his eventual release, he would be asked to lead a
life that honored his Savior and Lord.

While in the Virginia State Penitentiary, Harry was faithful
to his Bible readings, always completing the lessons from
Scripture that his friend and mentor, Bill Simmer, had been
sending him. He was also a faithful listener to *The Hour of
Decision,* Billy Graham's radio ministry. Desperately wanting
to draw closer to his God, Harry hoped the messages he'd
hear in the prison chapel would help him grow in Christ. But
such was not to be, as Harry remembers. "I went to only one
prison chapel service, and I have no idea what Bible the chaplain used," he says. "I just knew he wasn't using mine. I sensed
no fellowship in that place, and hardly any volunteers ever
came to preach, sing, or pray for the prisoners." Meanwhile,
Harry did his best to share his faith with a hardened group of
convicts who were his constant companions. Few were eager
to listen. Fewer yet chose to accept the freedom found in a
relationship with Jesus Christ.

**Harry did his best to share his faith with
a hardened group of convicts,
who were his constant companions.
Few were eager to listen.**

Today there are many prison ministries throughout the
United States that are doing Christ-honoring work behind
bars, such as Bill Glass Ministries, Chuck Colson's Prison
Fellowship, The Salvation Army, International Prison Ministry
(Chaplain Ray), and Good News Jail & Prison Ministry. Daily,

these five ministries are touching the lives of prisoners and their families and are helping to bring spiritual hope to thousands each year. In fact, according to the Institute for Prison Ministries at the Billy Graham Center at Wheaton College, there are approximately 450 to 500 jail and prison ministries across the country. Many are small; most are a one- or two-person operation. But whether the ministry is large or small, God is touching the hearts of people to support these groups as chaplains and volunteers go into our prisons to share His news of spiritual healing to men and women behind bars.

When Harry was serving his time, effective prison ministries for our nation's prisoners were few and far between. But Harry knew nothing about ministry statistics back then; all he knew—or needed to know—was that Chaplain Bill never forgot about his son in the faith, Harry Greene. *Never.*

Harry likens visits from Bill to "manna from heaven." He says, "Bill encouraged me, loved me, and helped me up when I was down. Now, as we write the words in this chapter, I have just received word that Bill's precious wife, Helen, has gone to be with her Lord, whom she loved so much. I learned that shortly before the end, Bill told Helen he loved her and asked her if she could see the angels. Helen weakly said yes, and passed on to Glory. When I visited with Bill and Helen only a month ago, I was stunned at how the cancer had ravaged her and how weakened her condition had become. However, I was also amazed at her alertness, and I shall always treasure those hours we spent together—for some special reasons.

"You see, on December 7, 1965, I was released from prison, and that same night Helen welcomed me to her dinner table as if I were her long-lost son. This wonderful, gracious, godly lady became like a second mother to me, and I have loved her and appreciated her for her compassion and understanding all these years. I thank God that He gave me that last afternoon with her so I could tell her how much God had used her to bless me."

When the time came for Harry to leave and return to Richmond, Helen said she wanted to talk to him alone. The cancer had ruined her throat, and she could speak only in a hoarse whisper.

Harry says, "Helen and I were alone for about fifteen minutes, and I had to lean in closely to hear and understand her. She said several things to me of a personal nature, which I shall always treasure. Then Helen whispered, 'Harry, never take your eyes off God. Keep the vision going and trust in Him for all things. He always blessed Bill and me, and He will always be there for you. We are so pleased at how the ministry has grown, but what really blesses us is how many people are coming to Christ. Please tell all our chaplains to never give up.'

"Even knowing she only had a few days left, sitting there in her easy chair, fading in and out of consciousness, her thoughts were clear, and her charge to me was such a blessing that I know I will never forget that quarter of an hour I spent with as godly a woman as I ever hope to meet."

> **"Helen whispered, 'Harry, never take your eyes off God. Keep the vision going and trust in Him for all things. He always blessed Bill and me, and He will always be there for you.'"**

Harry says that Bill and Helen always seemed to know what he was going through, always ministering to him in accordance with the words of Psalm 146:7: "Which executeth judgment for the oppressed: which giveth food to the hungry. The LORD looseth the prisoners." "Helen, I dedicate this chapter to you because of what you and Bill meant to me during those long, dark days when I was paying my debt to society," Harry says. "I'm not ashamed to tell you that tears fall from my eyes as I remember all of God's faithful servants who've gone home to be with their Savior, especially those whose hearts were committed to sharing Jesus Christ with men and women behind bars."

Finally, the day came when Harry's time in the Richmond State Penitentiary ended. He had completed his sentence, and with $25 in the pocket of a state-issued green suit and purple tie, Harry took one step closer to freedom. But, as Harry says, "Being released didn't make too much difference, because I walked right out of the door of the penitentiary and got into a Washington, D.C., police squad car and was driven to the general jail in the District of Columbia, where I was ready to start the whole process all over again. I had served my time in Virginia, but warrants had also been served on me from the District of Columbia and Prince George's County in Maryland. Because I had been charged in those jurisdictions, I also had to face charges there. At times I wondered, *would it ever end?*"

"At times I wondered, *would it ever end?*"

This time, at least, it wasn't prison. Harry was booked into the D.C. jail and was assigned to a dormitory that housed approximately 250 inmates. Once again, Harry was the new guy in a hostile environment. His court date was scheduled for the next day. As he entered his cell, a large inmate approached Harry and said, "It would be a good idea if you just laid down on your bunk and stayed there, okay?" Harry did what he was told. He lay down on his bunk and stayed there. He remembers, "I was not about to get up and go anywhere. About the only motion I dared to make that night was to relieve myself in a cup. But I never slept. I never even got off my bunk. Here I was, a prisoner supposedly toughened by doing hard time in the state pen, and I didn't dare get off my bunk."

The next day in court Harry pled guilty, and the judge sentenced him to another two years. But the judge suspended the sentence, provided Harry serve a year on parole without further crimes. He signed all the parole papers, walked out of that court room, and got in a Prince George's County, Maryland, police car. Harry was driven to Prince George's County to the Upper Marlboro Jail, where he remained for five days.

"On the fifth day," Harry recalls, "I received a sentence to run concurrent with the District of Columbia's, and I walked out a free man. My ordeal was over. And in case you wondered who might have been there to pick me up upon my release, it was Chaplain Bill Simmer. Once again, Bill was there for me. The date of my release was December 7, 1965."

Praising the Lord together, Bill drove Harry to visit pastor Butch Hardman at Barcroft Bible Church in Arlington, Virginia. Bill knew how important it was for Harry to connect immediately with a pastor and other evangelical Christians who would encourage him in his faith. Harry also recognized that if he was going to make it on the outside, he would need meaningful Christian fellowship as soon as possible. The seed for Harry's future spiritual growth had now been planted. After leaving the pastor's office, Bill and Harry drove to Bill's home—which was also the location of the headquarters of the fledgling jail and prison ministry, housed on Bill's property in the back of a converted garage.

As they drove to Bill's house, Harry was thinking, *Man, I've been locked up for two years, and all I'm thinking about is how I want to go to a movie, or go to McDonald's, or do something that I haven't done for nearly two years.* "So while I'm making all these grandiose plans to spend the next few days having a good time, Bill turns to me and says, 'Okay, Harry, we've got to build your bedroom.' I said, 'What? Build my bedroom? What about the movie, and the McDonald's hamburger, and . . .' But Bill says, 'That's right, Harry, I'm converting the basement of the house into a halfway house for ex-offenders, and you're our first guest!'

"Suddenly nobody was telling me I had to come back in, no one was saying I had to go to bed, no one was telling me when or what to eat."

"Before I knew it, Bill had a couple of guys come over to start building and painting, and by nightfall, amazingly, my room was livable. Then I started thinking: *I've come out of one prison and entered another.* But once the dust settled and the paint dried, I realized I was wrong, because that night, for the first time in a long time, I realized this was no prison at all. It was true freedom. I left my new quarters, walked out to the street, and took a long walk. I looked up at the stars, and I watched the people going by. The *world* was passing before my eyes, and suddenly nobody was telling me I had to come back in, no one was saying I had to go to bed, no one was telling me when or what to eat, when to take a shower, when to do this, when to do that. I began to understand how institutionalized I had become. I also started to realize that I really was free, and that if I wanted to walk across the street, I could go and not worry about being shot. If I wanted to run until I dropped, that was okay. If I wanted to get on the bus and take a ride, it was okay. I no longer had to watch my back.

Suddenly, I was experiencing the kinds of things most of us take for granted—*like the freedom to do anything we want.*"

That night, as Harry puts it, his life was restored. "Just to walk out under God's clear sky was a tonic to my soul and to my spirit," he recalls. "To look up into the heavens and see my breath in the coldness of the night—and to keep taking long, deep breaths of air—was one of the most exciting and emotional moments of my life."

Then, as if coming from nowhere, Harry began to recite the comforting words of Psalm 23:

> The LORD is my shepherd; I shall not want. He maketh me to lie down in green pastures: he leadeth me beside the still waters. He restoreth my soul: he leadeth me in the paths of righteousness for his name's sake. Yea, though I walk through the valley of the shadow of death, I will fear no evil: for thou art with me; thy rod and thy staff they comfort me. Thou preparest a table before me in the presence of mine enemies: thou anointest my head with oil; my cup runneth over. Surely goodness and mercy shall follow me all the days of my life: and I will dwell in the house of the LORD for ever.

Suddenly, the words of Proverbs 14:12 also rushed to Harry's consciousness, the verse God had used to get his attention while in jail: "There is a way which seemeth right unto a man, but the end thereof are the ways of death."

Harry knew quite a lot about the "reprobate" mind. He had nursed his own for years.

One by one, the Lord packed powerful passages of Scripture into Harry's receptive heart, including one from

Full Pardon

Romans 1:28: "And even as they did not like to retain God in their knowledge, God gave them over to a reprobate mind." Harry knew quite a lot about the "reprobate" mind. He had nursed his own for years. He could have written a manual on how to seer one's conscience, live for oneself, and pretend there is no God. Yet, his rebellion from the Father—and his obstinate rejection of the faith of his childhood—had only given him time behind bars. Now, as he walked the streets of freedom on that crisp December night, his mind's eye could see the hundreds of men with whom he'd done time. He could see their angry faces, the hatred in their eyes, and the fear in their hearts; he could also see and feel their *reprobate minds.*

Today, Good News chaplains continue to go one-on-one with these same reprobate minds in the same kinds of jails and prisons here at home and around the world. Harry says, "Our chaplains work with thousands of former Harry Greenes every day, and they do it with love and compassion whether the prisoners come to faith in Christ or not. That's because it's not about numbers; *it's about being faithful to our calling to share the Good News with those behind bars.* We are only witnesses to Christ's grace and favor; the Holy Spirit changes a man or woman's life. Right now, I can take you across this country and introduce you to bankers and lawyers and doctors and preachers and housewives and pillars of society whose lives were turned around in a jail or prison because a Good News chaplain brought the Word of God to them."

While in those jails and prisons, the chaplains regard everyone in that facility as someone who needs to establish a love relationship with Jesus Christ—including staff and administration. Over the years, the chaplains have led sheriffs, police chiefs, judges, probation officers, wardens, and correctional officers to Christ, "and that's the way it should be," Harry says. "You cannot leapfrog the spiritual needs of the corrections staff to get to inmates to talk to them about Jesus. This group of men and women also needs the saving message of Jesus Christ. That's because degenerate minds are not only caged behind bars. We all have them. And that's why we all need a Savior, just as I needed a Savior. That's why Good News keeps doing what we do day after day, 365 days a year. It's our calling. It's what God has commanded us to do."

Night had now fallen, and it was time for Harry to return to his newly constructed bedroom—fresh paint smells and all. As he retraced his steps on that crisp December night, returned to Bill's house, and went to sleep (with the light on) that first night of freedom in more than two years, he said to himself, *Now that I'm out, I promise to go straight. With God's help and the encouragement of my Savior and Lord, Jesus Christ, I will go straight.*

"As I look back on my life at the time," Harry says, "I fully realize the one person I had been cheating most was the man who, every day, had been staring at me in the mirror—a theme an anonymous poet has penned better than I could ever express it":

> When you get what you want in your struggle for self,
> And the world makes you king for a day,
> Just go to a mirror and look at yourself,
> And see what that man has to say.

> For it isn't your father or mother or wife,
> Whose judgment some day you must pass;
> The fellow whose verdict counts most in your life,
> Is the one staring back from the glass.

> Some people may think you're a straight-shooting chum,
> And call you a wonderful guy,
> But the man in the glass says you're only a bum,
> If you can't look him straight in the eye.

Full Pardon

He's the fellow to please, never mind all the rest,
For he's with you clear to the end,
And you have passed your most dangerous, difficult test,
If the man in the glass is your friend.

You may fool the whole world down your pathway of years,
And get pats on the back as you pass,
But your final reward will be heartache and tears,
If you've cheated the man in the glass.

In the late 1950s, God gave Chaplain Bill Simmer the vision to minister to men and women behind bars. For the next twenty-four years, Bill and Helen Simmer poured their lives into what later became Good News Jail & Prison Ministry. In 1983 Bill relinquished leadership of the growing organization to his "son in the faith," Harry L. Greene, current president of the ministry.

As you have learned so far from Harry's story, he continues to remain deeply indebted to Chaplain Bill for always "being there" when he needed a friend and counselor most. Today, from one man with a vision from God, Bill Simmer, and from one jail in Fairfax, Virginia, the ministry of Good News has grown to encompass chaplains throughout the United States and overseas. By the end of the year 2001, based on current requests, Good News anticipates it will be in more than two hundred institutions, ministering to an average daily inmate population of over 100,000.

These chaplains provide pastoral care to anyone in their prison "flock" who desires it. It was Chaplain Bill's unselfish, ever-present caring and compassion that made all the difference in the world for Harry Greene while he was in jail and prison, and especially as he faced the many challenges that lay ahead as he returned to society.

Chapter 9

Reaching Out to Those People

> When we draw our final breath, the question will
> not be who we are but who we've been.
> Not how much we've got, but how much we've given.
> Not if we've won, but if we've run.
> Not if we were a success, but if we were a servant.
>
> *Woodrow Kroll, Back to the Bible*

Once an inmate is released from prison—especially after a lengthy incarceration—there is always a tendency to speak louder than normal. Harry remembers how he would virtually shout at people in what should have been quiet conversations. "Jails are loud, noisy, unsettling places, with prisoners yelling, loudspeakers blaring, and the sounds of iron doors opening and closing throughout the day and night," he says. "I guess I was always compensating for the distractions that had surrounded me by raising my voice, even though I didn't know I was doing it. I just got used to talking more loudly than I normally would, a pattern than continued for some time even after I was released. To say nothing of the light I left *on* in my bedroom at night for weeks. I'm sure much of my behavior seemed strange to many people, but most seemed to understand that I needed time to adjust to the outside world—and it *was* an outside world, foreign as night and day from prison."

One of the major adjustments for Harry would be to learn how to become a responsible person within the context of his new freedom. He had to learn how to work, earn his own way, pay his debts, treat people with respect, be a decent citizen, and leave his conning ways behind—none of which would necessarily come easy to someone who had just spent a good portion of his young life behind bars. Harry says, "To become a responsible person demands a commitment and a decision. One of the reasons we have so much recidivism today—men, women, and young people who return to prison again and again—is that folks simply refuse to change from the inside *on their own*. They may have changed some of their behavior, as far as an institution is concerned, by showing up for self-improvement classes, completing educational courses, and even receiving graduate degrees. But inside, if they're still the people they always were, nothing really changes. That's why 70 to 80 percent of all inmates will leave prison and, within a relatively short time, will commit new crimes, be arrested, and return to incarceration. Simply educating a prisoner—as important as education is—does not make an inmate a better person any more than unbridled success makes a person kind. Change comes from within."

> **"Seventy to 80 percent of all inmates will leave prison and, within a relatively short time, will commit new crimes, be arrested, and return to incarceration."**

Harry was aware of the work that was cut out for him. He knew Jesus Christ had changed his heart; he also knew he would need to demonstrate to others that he could be a responsible human being—something he hadn't been known for prior to going to prison. He didn't know how it would all work out; he just knew he'd have to earn people's trust. In the meantime, he wondered, would people accept him? Or would they see him as a second-class citizen because he was an ex-con? How would he be able to withstand whatever rejection he might face? If confronted, would he revert to his old patterns? Or would his faith in Christ be strong enough to carry him through? All questions to which he did not know the answers—but would soon find out.

Harry says, "The very day I was released from prison, a body of believers reached out to me in full acceptance as a brother in Christ. I was blown away. *Did they really know what they were doing? I mean, come on, I had just been released from prison! I had done hard time. How could they possibly trust the likes of me? I'd conned people in the past; how did they know I wouldn't do it again?* But the other shoe never dropped. It was amazing! A former Youth for Christ director in the area was pastor of the church I began to attend and, oddly enough, was the first congregation to support the ministry of Good News. It was the church Bill and Helen Simmer had attended while going to Washington Bible College."

As you will recall, Harry knew all about church. Attendance pins for perfect attendance had been a hallmark of his younger days. Trouble was that he was never a follower of Jesus. Now he was an ex-convict Christian, starting over—from scratch. Harry recalls those first few days of freedom. "Bill Simmer took me to see the pastor Rev. Marlin C. 'Butch' Hardman, who said two things to me: one, that the entire church body had been praying for me while I was in prison; and two, that they were willing to accept me into the congregation with open arms. I cannot tell you what those words from the pastor's mouth did for me. I was speechless. *Me? They accepted me? Why? How could they accept me without even knowing me?* I was overwhelmed by their love and acceptance."

Yet today, such acceptance is more the exception than the rule. So many of God's people continue to be reticent about welcoming a former inmate into their fellowship, too often seeing them as *one of those people*—men and women who, because of bad decisions, are somehow destined to live at the bottom of the social and spiritual ladder for the rest of their lives. Well, Harry can tell you a story about one of *those people*.

"A young soldier fighting in the swamps during the Vietnam War was wounded and was returned to a military hospital in Hawaii for rehabilitation and treatment. As soon as he was able, he called his parents from his hospital bed to tell them he was injured but that he would be all right in time. His parents rejoiced at the news.

"So many of God's people continue to be reticent about welcoming a former inmate into their fellowship."

"'Mom and Dad,' he said, 'the even better news is that I think I'll be coming home soon.'

"'Oh, Son, we're so happy. Just tell us when you'll be arriving, and we'll be there to celebrate the great day of your return home,' said his parents.

"'And, by the way,' said the young soldier, 'I've met a friend here named John, and John is a guy I'd like to bring along home with me.'

"'Son, nothing would give us greater pleasure than to meet one of your fellow soldiers. By all means, bring him with you, and we'll celebrate your safe arrival together.'

"'But, Mom and Dad, I need to tell you something,' said the young man.

"'What's that?' said his folks.

"'You see, my friend John doesn't have a left leg or a left

arm. He stepped on a land mine in Vietnam and it blew them off. But he is as bright as he can be, and all his mental faculties are there. He's been a great friend to me, even though he doesn't get around very easily.'

"Silence on the other end of the phone.

"After a long pause, the young soldier's mother said, 'Uh, Son, you know, we don't have a very large house. And, well . . . well, your father and I will have to think about your bringing John home with you. We'll get back to you with our answer. Meanwhile, get well. We'll see you soon.'

"A few days later the soldier called back and told his parents how well he was doing, that he was making exceptional progress, and that he'd soon be able to return home. Then he asked, 'By the way, have you thought about John? Would it be okay if he comes home with me?'

"'Son, you know we love you, but your father and I have talked about it, and, well, you know, *those people* are so hard to care for. They disrupt the lives of regular people, and, well, they are just so difficult to deal with. I hope it's okay if we just celebrate your return. Perhaps John could come visit some time in the future. We'd love to meet him, but we don't think it would be a good idea right now. I think you understand as well as anyone how difficult it is to deal with *those people*.'

"'Okay,' he said, with a tear in his voice. 'I understand. Perhaps another day. Yes, another day would be fine. Bye, Mom and Dad. I love you.'

"Two days later, there was a knock on the door of the young soldier's home. A colonel stood there with hat in hand, announcing that the woman's son had committed suicide in his hospital in Honolulu. Grief-stricken, the boy's mom and dad wondered if they could ever cope with the tragedy—especially when all seemed to be going so well.

"A few days later, when the body arrived home in its casket, the parents opened it to view their son's remains and pay their final respects. To their shock, they saw their son had no left leg and no left arm. And then it hit them like a mountain of bricks: their boy had been one of *those people*—just like the others for whom they had so little time. Their pain was immediate and long lasting: because of their lack of love and acceptance, they had lost their young soldier forever. He had been one of *those people.*

"And so it goes in our own lives: we all have *those* in our experience whom we seem to think God either cannot save, or *those people* we should simply not bother ourselves with. They're disruptive. They mess up our carefully laid plans. Too many need disabled parking, drive too slowly, are too old, too young, too right-wing, too left-wing, always *too something. Those people* slow us down and keep us from moving at our usual pace.

"Unfortunately, most former inmates are also seen as *those people,* even by Christians. However, while too many churches have not yet come to accept such individuals, I thank God for those congregations that stand with us as partners in ministry to *those people.*"

> "Unfortunately, most former inmates are also seen as *those people,* even by Christians."

So Harry has this personal charge to you. "If you believe that Jesus Christ is the answer and that only He can change a life, then I hope you also believe in your heart that we can ill afford to refer to any former prisoner as one of *those people,* but instead see these men, women, and children as deeply loved and accepted by the Father—and therefore worthy of our acceptance as well. This is both the attitude and the calling of Good News Jail & Prison Ministry: we are all fellow beggars telling others where to find bread—the Bread of Life. Because the ground is always level at the foot of the cross."

* * * *

When Harry inhaled his first exhilarating breaths of freedom that day of his release, he vowed he would never go back to prison. Never! "The only way they would ever get me back behind bars was feet first," he says. "I'd been there, done that, and I was determined never to sit in a prison cell again. That's why I can say that other than my salvation, the greatest decision I ever made was not to leave God hanging on a hook when I left prison. *I took him with me, and He's been with me ever since.* Not that it's been easy. If I were to draw two lines that reflect my life from the day I left prison to today, with God on one line, and Harry on another, God's line would be straight as an arrow. There would be no deviation; you could plumb it forever, and it would never budge."

But Harry's line? "Well, that would be a different kind of line—sort of a jagged representation of a series of seismic disturbances, where it goes way right, then way left, but a line that eventually comes back to parallel with God's line," he says. "That's because a gracious Heavenly Father continues to draw me back to Him when I mess up, when I make bad decisions, and when I exhibit the qualities of an unfaithful servant. Yet, despite my unfaithfulness, God has always been there for me. I certainly don't feel I have any more of a personal relationship with God than anyone else does, and I don't think there's anything all that special about me. But I do know what God took me through, and I know He sought me out and rescued me with a loving hand that I felt on my shoulder from the first day of my conversion."

Full Pardon

It was a condition of Harry's parole that he find a job immediately, something he was eager to do. Fortunately, Jesse Bell, a member of the Good News Mission Board of Trustees, owned a moving and storage company, an agent of North American Van Lines. He agreed to interview Harry for possible employment—at Bill Simmer's request.

> **"I just believe in giving a man a second chance. But you'll need to start at the bottom by lifting boxes and loading trucks— for fifty dollars a week."**

The day of the interview arrived, and Mr. Bell peered at Harry from the other side of his desk. "Harry," he said, "I don't care what you've done in the past. I just believe in giving a man a second chance. But you'll need to start at the bottom by lifting boxes and loading trucks—for fifty dollars a week."

"That's fine with me Mr. Bell," Harry responded. "I just appreciate you giving me a chance."

Yes, it was a job, but it was also a nasty reduction in wages for a man who was accustomed to having hundreds, even thousands, of dollars in his pocket. "The fact that I was able to accept being humbled by such a low salary seemed to prove that I had gone through a change in mind-set," Harry says. "I knew I had no choice but to accept the job and the money. I knew I had to do whatever I needed to do in order not to return to prison—and *I was not going to return to prison.*"

This would be Harry's first job since beating the drums at one of his old watering holes. Harry started work on December 13, 1965. As Mr. Bell had promised, Harry was soon lifting heavy boxes and loading trucks—for fifty dollars a week. Soon, however, Harry discovered a quality in Jesse Bell that exceeded the role of employer; he had found a mentor, counselor, and someone who would become a lifelong friend. In the weeks that followed, it was older men such as Bill Simmer, Pastor "Butch" Hardman, and Jesse Bell who helped nurture and mentor Harry in his new faith. Even the brother-in-law of the pastor, J. David Holden, president of a local bank, got involved and would be the first person to give Harry a loan. Mr. Holden was also willing to give a man a second chance, something he demonstrated by watching Harry sign his first loan document, knowing full well the young man had a history of writing hundreds of bogus checks and using aliases too numerous to mention. Harry smiles now and says, "It really is true that God works in mysterious ways. Why else would responsible business people trust an ex-con!"

Harry waited for the day when someone in the church would finally throw his past up to him, but that day never came.

The next several months were important for Harry's spiritual growth. He enjoyed regular counseling sessions with Chaplain Simmer, participated in Bible studies, and ate most of his meals with Bill and Helen. Church life, however, was more difficult for Harry, since he suffered from paranoia not uncommon to most released prisoners. Harry felt people were starring at him, eyeing him suspiciously, wondering if he would go straight. After all, everyone in the church knew of his criminal background, so they would be more than justified in scrutinizing his every move. Harry waited for the day when someone in the congregation would finally throw his past up to him, but to his surprise that day ever came. He received nothing but love and acceptance from his brothers and sisters in Christ. But the best was yet to come, for God would give Harry both a surprise and a blessing in the person of Barbara Lee Warfield.

Barbara held the position of head cashier at the State Department; she also volunteered to work several nights a week doing bookkeeping for Good News. Harry remembers, "I found out that Barbara went to the same church that I had just attended, and I learned we would be in the same Sunday school class the following Sunday. Now you've got to understand, I had never dated a practicing Christian woman in my life! So there I was, hemming and hawing about how I was going to get up the nerve to ask her out. It was during the holidays, and I knew the Sunday school class was about to have a Christmas party—perfect for a first date, I thought. Since there would be a large group of people at the party, I figured she wouldn't feel threatened by being seen with an ex-convict. I asked Bill for Barbara's phone number. Well, he gave me her number—but it was an old one that was no longer valid. I learned later that Bill wanted to buy a little extra time so he could talk to Barbara first!

"So here I am, calling this number night and day and not getting any answer. In the meantime, Bill tells Barbara he knows I want to ask her to go to the Sunday school Christmas party, and, if she wants to go with me, that she should appear at the house on Saturday morning, using some lame excuse for stopping by—like dropping off a file or something. Bill knew I'd be home doing some chores. If Barbara came by, it meant she wanted to go out with me."

Sure enough, Barbara stopped by on Saturday morning carrying a little manila folder. Later, Harry found out there was nothing in it!

"Barbara, how would you like to go to the Sunday school Christmas party with me?" Harry asked her.

Barbara hesitated a few seconds—which seemed like minutes to Harry—and then said, "Yes, I guess so."

"You could have knocked me over with a very small feather," Harry recalls. "Chaplain Bill had played cupid, and I was glad he did, because God blessed our courtship from day one, and by the time February rolled around, I had asked Barbara to marry me."

Harry, however, had a little problem. He needed to buy Barbara a ring, but he didn't have any money. So the couple went to a Kay Jewelers in Arlington to see what they had to offer.

"I can still see the face of the sales lady who approached me and said, 'Can I help you, sir?'" Harry recalls. "I was considering asking her for credit, but I didn't know how to go about it. Meanwhile, the lady helped Barbara pick out a ring she liked, one that was fairly inexpensive—around three hundred dollars, I think—but still a healthy stretch for my thin wallet. I knew I had to do something fast, so I said I wanted to talk to the manager. 'Is there a problem?' asked the sales lady. 'No,' I said. 'I just need to see the manager before we go any further.'"

> ## "Chaplain Bill had played cupid, and I was glad he did, because God blessed our courtship from day one."

The manager, Mr. Levy, emerged from his office and leaned casually on the glass counter that displayed an assortment of watches, bracelets, and rings. "Yes, how may I help you?" he asked.

Harry replied, "I'm Harry Greene, and this is my fiancée, Barbara Warfield. We're planning to get married, and we've come in to select a ring."

"Well, that's great! What may I show you?"

At this point Harry started to sweat. "Well, you see, I'm . . . I'm an ex-convict, and I just got released from prison in December. I don't have any credit, and I need you to extend it to me."

The manager backed up a bit, and then he backed up some more. Then, an increasingly troubled Mr. Levy backed up some more. "I could tell by the color that was quickly leaving his face that he didn't know what to say—or do," Harry remembers. "He just stood there, as if in a trance. He looked at me, and then he looked at Barbara, then he looked at me again, sizing me up. Suddenly, out of his mouth came the unexpected words, 'Well, you know, I've never had anyone say that to me before. But because of your honesty, I'm going to give you credit. After all, if this woman believes in you, why shouldn't I!' That experience was pivotal in the restoration of my life."

Mr. Levy, a total stranger, believed in Harry because of his honesty. It was almost more than the young ex-prisoner could handle, and *integrity* has been Harry's "middle name" ever since. In fact, whenever Harry gives his testimony, you will hear him say, "Early on in my conversion, God taught me the greatest thing I own is my integrity, and that if I lose or compromise that part of me, I have not only lessened my testimony, but I have also reduced my standing as a human being and as a man. That's why today, in all that I do, if I know there's a problem with someone, or if a friend, colleague, or neighbor has a problem with me, I go to that individual immediately. We just stop our business and get it taken care of on the spot. The thing that will get to me quicker than anything else is for someone to question either my integrity or the integrity of the ministry that God has given me to oversee."

"The three greatest gifts that God ever gave me have been my salvation, my wife, and my children."

Harry has often been asked, "What kind of a woman marries an ex-con?" He smiles and answers, "Well, you know, Barbara actually didn't trust me for about three years. She thought I was probably going to take her, use her, grab her money, and split, I guess. But I didn't take her money, I didn't use her, and I didn't leave. God just worked it all out. It's all I can say . . . *God just worked it out.* I know both Bill and our pastor talked to Barbara on several occasions, and I'm sure that helped her accept me and trust me—over time. However, I don't want to give the impression there were no rocky roads in our relationship, because there have been many. But God continues to navigate us through them, even as we remain faithful to one another.

"Today, in all sincerity, I can say the three greatest gifts that God ever gave me have been my salvation, my wife, and my children. If there is a fourth, I suppose it might be Mr. Levy—a frightened jeweler who chose, against all odds, to believe in me, when he could just as easily have kept backing away."

On June 17, 1966, Harry and Barbara were married at Barcroft Bible Church in Arlington, Virginia. Bill Simmer and Butch Hardman performed the ceremony, and Harry's best man was his employer, Jesse Bell. It was a joyful day, especially for Harry's parents, William and Maggie Mae Greene, and for Harry's grandmother, Kitty Sullivan—the former missionary to

Alaska who had never stopped praying for Harry.

Immediately, Barbara began to exert a profound influence on Harry as she helped him mature and accept increasing amounts of responsibility as a husband. She taught him the meaning of a good marriage and quality interpersonal communication, and she stuck with him when he was down or going through hard times. She was—and is—a faithful wife, always there to uplift Harry when things got rough. And things did get rough.

Several months after their marriage, Harry's parents were divorced. While Harry's imprisonment undoubtedly contributed to the demise of his parents' relationship, it was also evident that the problems within their marriage stretched back many years. As with all divorce, it brought with it a terrible sense of loss. Harry and Barbara were determined, before God, that it would never happen to them—a promise that would take on special importance in the years ahead as a ministry larger than themselves would one day become their passion . . . as God would help them discover their spiritual gifts . . . and as they would spend their lives developing such gifts, learning that life has significance only when those gifts are used for the eternal benefit of *those people.*

A True Story from the Files of
Good News Jail & Prison Ministry

"Nigel, why are you hanging around with those boys? You're gonna get in trouble someday if you keep runnin' with the wrong crowd."

"Aw, Mom, give it a rest. I know what I'm doing. I'm young; I'm not gonna get hurt," said the boy defiantly.

Nigel equated youth with invincibility, but a bullet in the head proved him wrong! Nigel survived the shootout but was left with a large piece of lead lodged in his skull that reminded him of his mortality. When he got out of the hospital, he was placed behind bars on a murder charge. It was the first time he'd been in any institution, and it was a rude awakening. "I didn't do nothin' wrong!" Nigel fumed.

One day, a volunteer came to visit Nigel. As he listened, his mother's words came back to him. Nigel began thinking, *Maybe I did do something wrong, and that's why I'm here.*

Shortly after, Nigel committed his life to Christ, and although he now had a relationship with his Lord, he still struggled with anger. As Nigel described his aggressive feelings to our Good News chaplain, the chaplain listened, and then spoke.

"Nigel, living the Bible isn't about being a wimp, but there are different ways to be strong. It's easy to lose your cool and just hit someone, but it takes a bigger man to handle it verbally. I know what you're thinking: *This guy doesn't know what he's talking about.* Well, I spent some time in jail and God changed me. He can change you."

Today, Nigel has grown strong in following Christ's example. But there are tens of thousands more prisoners like Nigel who've not heard that God loves them.

When you share your resources with the ministry of Good News, you help us reach men and women who've made wrong decisions and placed themselves behind bars. Good News Jail & Prison Ministry is *your* ministry—and your opportunity to help see more lives changed for eternity through the power and love of the Person of Jesus Christ.

Chapter 10

Passing the Mantle

A good leader takes a little more than his share of the blame, and a little less than his share of the credit.

oon after Barbara and Harry were married, the young groom was promoted to claims manager at the trucking company, a position he held for about eighteen months. He later went into sales with the organization, became sales manager, and, in 1973, took over as president and co-owner with his brother, Dennis.

Meanwhile, God was doing great things at Good News, where Harry always seemed to find himself in the middle of the action. He says, "Bill Simmer was my spiritual father while I was in prison, and upon my release, our friendship only became stronger, especially as we would travel together to speak in churches, schools, and wherever I had an opportunity to give my testimony of the grace of God in my life. During this time, I was also learning the fine art of fund-raising, a skill I would need to perfect in the years to follow."

By now, Good News was becoming well known within the Washington area and was just starting its expansion to other parts of the country. Bill Simmer had started the ministry in Fairfax, Virginia, in 1961, later enlarging it to Alexandria, then to Arlington, and then on to Prince George's County and Montgomery County in Maryland—all suburbs of Washington, D.C. Then with both a spiritual leap of faith and a physical leap of thousands of miles, Bill began a Good News ministry in Hawaii—where Good News chaplains continue to be engaged in vibrant ministry today. One of the fascinating things about Good News is that it has never grown or extended its influence based on five- or ten-year plans, nor has it ever restricted its growth because of geographical boundaries. It has expanded only as God has opened doors, and where He has provided men and women to be chaplains who are willing to raise their own support to minister in the jails and prisons within their communities.

"This is God's work, and we desire to be in the center of God's plan at all times."

Harry says with a smile, "If you look at how the ministry has grown in the past and continues to grow today, you could say, 'You know, this work doesn't seem to be all that well planned.' I guess I'd have to agree with you, to some degree. But we're not selling widgets. This is not a 'product' that relies on the slogans, one-liners, and market savvy of gurus on Madison Avenue. This is God's work, and we desire to be in the center of God's plan at all times. We don't want to be ahead of Him or behind Him, but rather in step with Him all the way. That's one of the reasons I believe we are seeing such tremendous growth in the ministry right now."

* * * *

The year was now 1972. By the time Mark Spitz had left Munich, West Germany, "Mark the Shark" had won seven gold medals and had established seven world records in every one of his seven events. Never before had any Olympian, in any sport, accomplished such an incredible feat. In that same year, the Volkswagen Beetle—once dubbed the ugliest car on the face of the earth—stunned the automotive world by becoming the best-selling car ever. Not to be outdone by sports figures or automobiles, 1972 also saw the release of an invention that would eventually find its way into the briefcases of men and women worldwide: the pocket calculator, invented by Texas Instruments. In that same year, Hollywood released *The Godfather,* a movie not so much about power itself but about the transfer of power, as it related the story of the fictional Corleone family and how the family's power transferred from the aging father, Don Vito Corleone (Marlon Brando), to son Michael (Al Pacino). Nineteen seventy-two was indeed an interesting year; for Harry Greene it would soon become even more interesting.

The young ex-prisoner had proved himself to be an honest, honorable citizen, faithful husband, and loyal friend. He had worked hard, moved up the ranks, and had assumed more and more responsibility in the world of business. He did not return to his life of crime, nor did he ever entertain such a foolish idea (and he never left Barbara—although she *did* give him her own "three years of probation"). Harry's "coming clean" was being noticed by everyone who knew him—especially by a group of citizens from northern Virginia, which was being influenced by Sheriff J. Elwood Clements, the law enforcement officer of Arlington County, where Harry had been locked up and where God entered his life. The sheriff believed in Harry and continued to lobby for a substantial number of citizens to come together to petition the governor for a full pardon on Harry's behalf. In October 1972, it actually happened. Harry L. Greene, former convict, received a pardon from Gov. Linwood Holton.

In October 1972, Harry L. Greene, former convict, received a pardon from Gov. Linwood Holton.

Full Pardon

Harry heaves a huge sigh when he talks about the importance of that day. "I knew my pardon was being worked on, but I didn't have any great sense of expectation, because the governor only grants two or three each year," he says. "I always figured it was all in the Lord's hands. If He wanted it to happen, it would happen. But as I think back on that momentous event in my life, I can say that I really had worked hard to prove that I was worthy, that I had integrity, that I was not the same person who had committed all those crimes. From that standpoint, my full pardon became a validation of my changed life. Still, because I'd done so many bad things, it's difficult to say whether or not I was worthy of such a pardon. But I'd be lying if I told you it wasn't one of the greatest experiences of my life. No doubt about it: receiving a full pardon was a blessing from the governor—and from my Heavenly Father."

A pardon is not something for which you can go down to some office and ask. You don't stand in line, take a number, and when your name comes up say, "Uh, may I please have a pardon?" It doesn't work that way. Others have to step forward on a former prisoner's behalf. You can imagine that Harry— now Harry the preacher, communicator, and ministry president—sees more than one sermon in what happened to him in February 1972. He says, "There really is an analogy there. Just as I could do nothing on my own to activate and receive a pardon from the governor, by the same token, I could do absolutely nothing to save myself from my many sins. No amount of penance would have done it, and no sudden flurry of 'good works' would have won my salvation. I received my cherished eternal life in Christ solely because of what my Savior did for me on the cross: He died in my place, so that I might gain everlasting life."

At the time of his pardon, Harry was becoming more and more involved in the Good News ministry, giving his testimony whenever he could, traveling throughout the country, speaking at banquets, working with Bill Simmer, and always reminding his listeners that they, too, needed to receive God's merciful pardon in their own lives. "I loved what I was doing," he says, "and I sensed God was leading me to play a more active role when I was asked to be on the Board of Directors of the ministry. I remember that period of time well, because in 1973 our son, Matthew, was born. He was a special blessing to us, because for six years we had been unable to have children of our own, which was one of the most painful experiences of our married lives. We both wanted to raise a family that would be an honor to our Lord.

"'We're sorry, Mr. Greene, but you'll still need to move further from your past before you'll be able to adopt a child.'"

After so many years without children, Harry and Barbara had decided they would consult their doctors one more time, only to discover that a fertility problem was the culprit. Once they received that unhappy news, they made the decision to petition for adoption. Harry remembers, "We immediately approached an adoption agency, and everything was in order in our written documents, except for the small matter of my criminal record—even though I'd received a pardon. I was told, 'We're sorry, Mr. Greene, but you'll still need to move further from your past before you'll be able to adopt a child. Until that happens, we can't approve anything.' I wanted to tell them I was pedaling as fast as I could to remove myself from my former crimes, but instead just said, 'Well, I can understand how you feel about that.' However, I did ask them, 'Well, how far is *far?*' but did not receive an answer. They were basically saying, *Don't call us; we'll call you*—which, to me, meant, *Don't hold your breath.* We didn't."

Meanwhile, Harry and Barbara were made aware of the Holt Adoption Agency, which was then providing Eurasian children from overseas, primarily Southeast Asia, to American families. They were elated at the prospects of becoming adoptive parents, so they applied for a child and were accepted as potential adoptive parents. "There was great joy in the Greene household the day we received the official letter of acceptance from Holt," Harry recalls. "But that delight was tempered with another piece of good news: the same day we were accepted by Holt was the same day Barbara discovered she was pregnant with Matthew Wade—a little boy who quickly became the center of our life! For some reason known only to God, He had used His divine surgery to fix our fertility problems, because in 1977, I was present at the birth of our second child, Sara Elizabeth. Obviously, we no longer needed to adopt. As I've said before—and will continue to repeat until the day the Lord returns—the three greatest gifts that have ever come to Harry Greene have been my salvation, my wife, Barbara, and my precious children."

In addition to God's blessing in his personal life, Harry received a tremendous honor that illustrated the incredible grace of God. In 1982 Gov. Charles Robb appointed Harry to be the first ex-felon to serve on the Virginia State Board of Corrections. Four years later, Gov. Gerald Baliles appointed Harry to a second four-year term. A former inmate was now on the policy board that oversaw the very prison system in which he had been incarcerated!

By 1983 Harry was enjoying his best year in business, opening new accounts and anticipating a large income for the year as a result of his efforts. On top of the world, he wondered what else could possibly make him any happier. Once again, God took the reins of that question the day

Harry received a call from Helen Simmer. The physical and mental pressure, along with the stress of building and sustaining a ministry, had finally gotten to Harry's mentor. Being sensitive to the condition of its leader, the Good News Board granted Bill a leave of absence to rest and relax, hoping that some time away would put him back on top. However, even the R&R would not be enough respite for God's servant, and Bill realized it was time for him to step down from his leadership of Good News.

Harry remembers the phone call. "Bill was in Hawaii," he says. "He had called Helen, asking her to call me and say he felt the Lord wanted him to step down. I understood, and sensed he was making the right decision. In fact, I had actually already prepared my heart for this moment. What I was not prepared for was the next set of words to come out of Helen's mouth: 'Harry, Bill wants you to become the next president of Good News.' Now that was a good one, and I laughed uproarously. No way could I or would I do that—or so I thought. I had no formal religious training, no seminary education, and my short time in Bible college had been a bust. In my opinion, I had no qualifications whatsoever to assume the leadership of Good News. I protested and fussed for a few days, after which Bill cut me off and said, 'Look, Harry, the ministry doesn't need another preacher right now, but it does need a leader.' That caught my attention, and I said, 'Well, that's something I could probably do, but I just don't think it's something I'd be interested in.'

"Bill said, 'Will you pray about it?'

"Well, when your spiritual father asks you to pray about something, you say you'll pray about it. In all honesty, however, I gave only lip service to my prayer. I was so convinced it would not even be an option. But I did pray, sort of. A short time later, I received another call, from Helen. 'Harry,' she said, 'Bill called me and told me about your conversation. He wants to know what you've decided.' Now I knew Bill was serious about the matter and that I really needed to go to the Lord to determine about whether the position might be the one for me.

Right away, Harry knew what he would do. He would start playing *Let's Make a Deal with God.*

Right away, Harry knew what he would do. He would start playing *Let's Make a Deal with God,* a Harry Greene version of the old television show *Let's Make a Deal,* with Monte Hall. "I played the game like this," Harry says. "I'd say, 'God, if You really want me to do this, then I expect You do *this.* If You don't want me to take the position, then see that 'this' doesn't happen. I was so determined not to assume the role of president of Good News that I figured I could stack the deck in my favor. After all, I was pretty good at cards while in jail and prison!"

But there was a problem: God kept coming up with iron-clad reasons for Harry to take the position. He just couldn't get ahead of God on this one. "However, I had yet another card up my sleeve—a really big fleece—and one I knew even God couldn't do," Harry says. There were twenty members on the Good News Board, so I said to Bill, 'Okay, here's the deal. If the Board votes unanimously for me to do this, then I will do it.' In my heart I knew the Board would never vote unanimously for me. Well, surprise, surprise, the Board voted unanimously for me to become the next president.

"I still see images in my mind of that day. One of the Board Members at the time was Grady Wilson of the Billy

Graham Evangelistic Association, and I'll never forget seeing Grady climb that long flight of stairs to the boardroom on the second floor to cast his vote. It was a steep, difficult set of steps, and Grady was having serious heart problems at that time. I could see him stop and rest every few seconds, catching his breath, wiping his brow, with Bill Simmer on his arm offering him support as the two of them negotiated their way slowly to the top of the stairs. When I saw what was happening, I found myself getting choked up as I realized Grady thought enough of me and my leadership abilities to struggle his way into the boardroom to cast his vote on my behalf. From that day forward, Grady became a special friend, and I always held him in highest regard."

Then there was Harry Greene: ex-con, businessman, *president-elect*.

The Board was an amazing group of people, the chairman being the former head of the U.S. Capital Police, a man of deep faith who had also served as a volunteer in the Maryland jails where Good News chaplains carried out their ministry. This exceptional Board was composed of doctors, parachurch leaders, pastors, and other highly educated people who had already made their marks in their respective professions. Then there was Harry Greene: ex-con, businessman, *president-elect*.

Still, the more Harry thought about it, the more ridiculous it seemed for him to be President of Good News. "Before the final vote by the Board that day, Barbara and I had already spent a long time talking about how my new position would affect our lives," Harry recalls. "It would mean more travel for me and less time with Barbara and the family, along with the other personal challenges that people on the road have to make to do their work. I was thirty-nine years old at the time, and Matt and Sara were still young. I kept asking myself whether it would be fair to leave the raising of the children to Barbara while I was off doing the Lord's work in prisons throughout the country.

"I'll never forget the night we prayed about the position. When we finished our prayer time, Barbara said, 'If this is what God wants you to do, I'll support you 100 percent.' At that moment I knew my 'make a deal' with God was over. Since that day, Barbara has never complained about my involvement in Good News, and she's never been angry, even when I would need to travel as much as six months out of the year— not even during those difficult times when my physical presence would have made her life a whole lot easier.

"Barbara, I know you'll be reading this, so let me tell you in print what I've said to you for all these years: *I love you, appreciate you, and realize this ministry would never be what it is today had you not supported me from day one. You have done a tremendous job in raising our children, and it's because of your influence that they, too, have come to know Christ as their Savior. I love you, Barbara. I love you.*

"And I also want to say a word to you, Matt and Sara. No dad could ever be more proud of his children. You are both college graduates, fine, mature adults, and you truly are our pride and joy in every way."

Since Harry had gone through his own prison experience, had proved himself responsible during his parole, had been fully pardoned, and had displayed the leadership qualities any responsible corporation would want in a leader, the Board knew it had chosen the right person. For too long, Harry had been one of *those people* in the minds of some people on the outside. That meant he knew firsthand how prisoners feel when they are released. He also knew their physical, social, and spiritual needs while they were on the inside.

> ## Harry's heart was still in prison as he saw the faces and felt the pain of those who were behind bars.

Harry indeed was the man for the job. So he took over where his friend and mentor, Bill Simmer, had left off. As he did, Harry's heart was still in prison as he saw the faces and felt the pain of those who were behind bars. Harry says, "It is so important that we look at people based on who they are at the time we're dealing with them, not at what they've done in the past. We've all heard it said that 'once a crook, always a crook; once a murderer, always a murderer; once a rapist, always a rapist.' That's not necessarily true. Yes, there are those who will get out and repeat their offenses—there's no doubt about that—and there are those who deserve to be locked up for the rest of their lives. However, if we truly believe that Christ can change people's lives, then it doesn't have to be only those who walk down an aisle in a beautiful cathedral or church auditorium to accept Christ who are saved.

"For example, people will still come up to me and say, 'Do you really think someone can accept Christ in jail or prison?' Now that gets me worked up, and I usually respond, 'Do you really think somebody can accept Christ in your church?' And they'll say, 'No, no that's not what I mean. I mean, how can you be sure the prisoner is really saved?' Well, I'm sorry, but I'm not going to let that person off the hook so easily, so I answer, 'I can be assured of a prisoner finding Christ if you can be assured the person who walked down the aisle of your church to the front last week and told the pastor he wanted to accept Christ is saved. That's all up to God. It's not up to me, to you, the pastor, or a Good News chaplain.' Whether a person is sincere in his or her decision is completely up to God. If the sinner is sincere, that life will show a change of some kind. I'm afraid it all goes back to the attitude we still have toward *those* people . . . and whether they're playing games with our chaplains or not. Hey, we all play games— every day of our lives. Only God will ever be able to sort out the sheep from the goats. It's not our job to judge the intent of others."

> **"Prison is this great depository of people from every walk of life—and they're all men and women who need a Savior and who need love, compassion, and understanding."**

Harry suggests that much of society's attitude toward those in jail and prison has been formed by Hollywood over the years, and that such a representation is not completely accurate. He reminds us, "I know firsthand that some of the people in jails and prisons are career criminals, but most of the inmates are just like the people down the street from where you and I live—people who've simply made bad choices and poor decisions. When I was in prison, I met military ranks from private to general, I met pastors, I met leaders of industry, bankers, and businessmen—all as fellow inmates. It wasn't just the dirty, no-good Harry Greenes, or the mafia toughs, or the big-time crooks who were in there. Prison is this great depository of people from every walk of life—and they're all men and women who need a Savior and who need love, compassion, and understanding. One thing they don't need is to be regarded as one of *those people."*

As Harry accepted the mantle of leadership for the ministry, he kept recalling that his faith in Christ was the one thing that had enabled him to adjust to freedom. His own experience behind bars was a daily reminder of what Good News was all about. "When I left prison, I made the decision not to leave God behind," he says. "I trusted Him to get me through my prison experience, and He never let me down. I also promised to trust Him from that moment on. As president, I would need to make sure that the bureaucratic affairs and the 'business' part of the ministry would not distract me from what I knew was most important: *seeing lives changed for eternity."*

"'Lord, do what You want to do with my life. Show me what I should do, and I promise to do it.'"

Now Harry was president of the ministry, and he reflected on the time when he thought God might be calling him to become a pastor. "When I got out of prison and started my life all over, I was really saying, 'Lord, do what You want to do with my life. Show me what I should do, and I promise to do it.'" Harry decided that he should probably become a pastor, so he enrolled in Washington Bible College the month after being released. "Well, that was a joke," Harry says. "The Lord made it patently clear that being a Bible scholar or preacher was not what I was supposed to do. In fact, it was one of the two or three times since leaving prison that I came close to hitting somebody. The potential victim was one of my professors at the school!"

At the time, Harry was living in the halfway house in Arlington, and the Bible college was on Rhode Island Avenue in Washington, D.C. He was enrolled in a challenging course on the Book of Hebrews and was preparing for a big exam. The class met at 7:30 A.M. Bill Simmer had worked with Harry all weekend, drilling him on his class notes. "I had the material down cold and was ready for the toughest questions the instructor could possibly throw my way," Harry recalls. "I decided I would get up early on Monday morning, drive in to town, grab a cup of coffee, review my notes, and be fresh and ready to take the exam. I left the halfway house at 6:15, since it would normally take thirty minutes to get to the school. But there was a wreck on the 14th Street Bridge, and by the time I got to the college and parked my car, the 7:30 bell had already rung. As I ran into the classroom, the professor looked at me and said, 'Sorry, you're late, and you can't take the test.' He never asked me why I was late. He never asked me anything. Earlier on I had already had some problems with his attitude, but this was the last straw. I came within inches of putting out his lights, especially as I reflected on the doubts he'd shared with me previously about the Good News Ministry. You know: *love me, love my dog.* Anyone who dared criticize Good News was going to get a fight from me."

Fortunately, God withheld Harry's hand from "rearranging the shape of the man's face," as he puts it. "I would have done him grievous harm had I hit him," Harry says. "Instead, I dropped my books on the floor, turned around, walked out of that classroom, and never went back. As I look back on that day, I know for sure that to 'become a pastor' was my decision, not God's. He had other things for me to do, and He had to get me out of an exam on the Book of Hebrews to get my attention. Those 'other things' would involve establishing relationships with the true heroes of Good News—our faithful, God-honoring chaplains who serve day after day in our nation's jails and prisons, and in institutions throughout the world."

He Wanted to Go Back to Jail

In the parking lot of one of our Southern jails was a sight that shocked even the most seasoned Correctional Official. In plain view a young man was breaking into a CO's car! A Deputy Sheriff was summoned and the young man was arrested.

Strangely, he did not try to run or explain his way out of the situation. He just stood against the car wearing a pair of sunglasses he had just stolen from the officer's car. As the CO and the sheriff talked, they soon realized that this young man wanted to be arrested and *wanted* to go to jail.

When he was booked into the jail and his record was pulled from the computer, authorities discovered that only two hours before the young man had been released from the very jail to which he was returning! This young prisoner had no job, no support system, and no family waiting for him. He was afraid that he would return to drugs and his criminal friends, so he sought the security of once again going behind bars.

So often, regenerated men and women coming out of our prisons and jails have no church to go to and, certainly, no one waiting for them at the front door. Too often they are viewed with suspicion—as people who will never change. We know that this is simply not true.

Good News chaplains across America do wonderful work by introducing incarcerated men and women to the message of deliverance through Jesus Christ. But so many of these released prisoners become discouraged when they cannot find a church or Christians to help and encourage them.

Whether you've done time or not, if you are facing discouragement in your life, let God use it to motivate you to two things: First, seek to encourage someone else spiritually. Second, be open to receive the support of another growing Christian. Consider these encouraging words from Galatians 6:10: "As we have therefore opportunity, let us do good unto all people, especially unto those who are of the household of faith."

Chapter 11

Heroes behind Walls:
A Salute to Good News Chaplains

*Remember them that are in bonds, as bound
with them; and them which suffer adversity,
as being yourselves also in the body.*
Hebrews 13:3

C rime rates continue to demonstrate what criminologists have been saying for many years: *prisons do not create positive changes in the lives of inmates.* In most cases, incarceration becomes the graduate school of crime, an unsavory outcome often compounded by overcrowded and understaffed facilities that offer little, if any, opportunity for the kind of programs that could even remotely turn a man or woman away from a life of crime. Tough prisoners prey on weaker ones; harassment, beatings, and homosexual attacks wear down a prisoner's ability and will to survive. Self-respect, self-discipline, and job skills are hard to come by.

Today, there are approximately two million people behind bars in the United States. The tragedy is that 70 to 80 percent are repeat offenders. By human standards, the present and future for those behind bars remains bleak—except for one powerful factor: *evangelical chaplains who give their lives to reach out to lost men and women in jails and prisons in the name of our Lord and Savior, Jesus Christ.* It is to such men and women that we dedicate this chapter—those Good News chaplains who serve as unsung heroes behind otherwise impenetrable jail and prison walls.

Harry remembers that were it not for his own "hero," Chaplain Bill Simmer, he might easily have returned to his life of crime upon release from prison. "Bill was my spiritual father," Harry says. "He hung in there with me. He saw an angry, young criminal who needed the grace of God to turn his life around. While I held him at bay for too long—as I continued to play cards day after day, wishing he'd just go away—Bill never quit on me. He kept showing up. He kept loving me, accepting me, always challenging me to take an honest look at what I was doing to my life. Without Bill's tenacity and love, who knows where I would be today? *Probably still in some penitentiary—or dead.* I'm happy to say that God continues to supply Good News Jail & Prison Ministry with chaplains who have the same spiritual courage and insight that Bill Simmer brought to the ministry those many years ago.

"Without Bill's tenacity and love, who knows where I would be today?"

"Now, it is a pleasure to introduce you to a few of these chaplains who exemplify the ministry's heroes behind prison walls."

THE STORY OF RICK SWEENIE

"When you're an addict, not only do you use the drugs, but the drugs use you. And was I used. Even before my nightmare began, I had made many bad choices. It all started at an early age in my hometown of Council Bluffs, Iowa, when I began running with the wrong crowd. This concerned my Christian mother, who always made sure I attended church. In contrast, my father was an alcoholic who had little interest in what I did. My home environment heated up to the point where, at age sixteen, I decided to split. Soon after, I took off for Columbus, Nebraska, where I spent a year with my grand-parents. My talent for making bad friends scored another point against me when I ended up in juvenile court on a burglary charge. I was placed on probation, an obligation I usually ignored.

"That day there were several of us waiting to shoot up for the first time."

"I moved back to Council Bluffs and was married at eighteen. When the courts found out my wife was pregnant, they let me off probation. I guess they thought marriage would settle me down and make me more responsible. Little did they know! My wife was expecting our second baby when I bumped into an old acquaintance from high school. He was a user, and he convinced me that if I tried drugs I would be in for a good time. I was scared and hesitant at first, but I finally gave in to peer pressure. My first experience was with LSD, and it wasn't good—just weird.

"Soon after, a friend convinced me to try the needle. That day there were several of us waiting to shoot up for the first time. I remember nobody wanted to be first, and we were all arguing about who should be last. The dealer laughed, saying that next time we'd all be arguing about who'd get to be first. He was right. From there I went downhill fast. I was hooked. I began dealing drugs to support my habit. Drugs seemed more important to me than anything now—*more important than my wife, my kids, or my user friends*. Everyone and everything took second place to drugs. I was twenty-three years old and my home, my life, everything was in shambles. When drugs use you, they steal it all. Even the thrill I felt when I first used was now beyond my grasp.

"My drug habit was now on the increase, and I should have died many times. It was only the grace of God that I did not. Once I got hold of a bunch of methamphetamine and lay awake for seven days without food or sleep. In this zombie-like state, I drove to Omaha with some friends to make a buy. To my dismay, the cops were watching the drug house. I got busted and spent three days in the county jail. In the middle of the first night, I was lying on my cot when I felt my heart beating slower and slower. It had almost stopped when I jumped up, grabbed the bars, and yelled for help. There was no one around.

"As I desperately clutched the bars, I felt my heartbeat return to normal. I tried to put the close call out of my mind as I waited in vain for my 'friends' to bail me out. I found out later they didn't show because they were too busy partying with my drug supply. Dad finally got me out in time to enjoy Thanksgiving dinner with my family. The next day, I returned to drugs.

"All I could do was cry out to God."

"I was miserable and I wanted to change my life. But I wanted to do it my way. When an old family friend reminded me of Jesus' love and His offer of salvation, I told him 'no thanks.' I didn't want to be known as some 'Jesus freak.' I didn't think I needed God's help to change. In the next year and a half, I was arrested two more times on a total of six felony charges. Getting arrested seemed to be the only thing I was good at, and I was getting sick and tired of it all. I finally realized I couldn't turn things around alone. I needed help. Memories came flooding back: church messages from long ago, the friend who cared about me and who tried to turn me to Christ, near misses with death, my broken family.

"All I could do was cry out to God. And in that cold, dark city jail on April 18, 1973, He answered me with His loving hand of forgiveness and salvation. As I began to recall the Bible verse I learned as a child, God made the experience personal to me: *For God so loved Rick Sweenie that He gave His only Son, that if Rick Sweenie believes in Him, he should not perish but have everlasting life* (see John 3:16). That wonderful day, I trusted Jesus Christ as my personal Savior and gave my life to Him. I was sentenced to five years in prison. But this time I wasn't alone, and that was comforting. Regular meetings with the prison chaplain and Bible studies with a Christian inmate group provided opportunities for my spiritual growth. I enjoyed God's further blessing by having to serve only one year behind bars. When my sentence was up, I went to a work-release program at a halfway house.

"God put His seal of the Holy Spirit upon my life."

"After my release, I had some trouble adjusting. I kept company with my old friends and didn't bother sharing the Lord with them. Predictably, I fell back to using again. I had to learn to avoid both old and new acquaintances who were users. I took this problem to the Lord in prayer, and He led me to a Bible-believing church where I met many new, wonderful friends. Several had backgrounds similar to mine. They cared about *me*, not my past. The church I attended held meetings for prisoners once a month in the Douglas County (Nebraska) Jail. It was through the church, and Good News Chaplain Bob Potter, that I became involved in the Good News Jail & Prison Ministry. Later I was privileged to become the Good News chaplain at the Pottawattamie County (Iowa) Jail. After having served as a chaplain in Iowa and Nebraska, I now serve the Lord as a regional director for Good News.

"On December 9, 1988, I gratefully received a full pardon from Governor Branstad of Iowa. He fixed the state seal upon the document that proclaimed my pardon. But what I am most thankful for is the pardon I received from God when I trusted Jesus Christ as my Savior. As Governor Branstad explained it to me, a pardon is 'just like it never happened.' God's pardon is like that, too, because the blood of Jesus Christ cleanses us from all sin (see 1 John 1:7). Jesus willingly took the punishment for my sins when He died on the cross. God showed that He accepted that payment of my sin debt when He raised Jesus from the dead. When I agreed with God by trusting Christ, God put His seal of the Holy Spirit upon my life (see Ephesians 1:13).

"As I look back on my life, it seems as though I was lost in a maze. The only way out was Jesus Christ, but I figured there had to be some other way. I tried everything but only found dead ends. When I faced the truth and realized I couldn't free myself, I was finally in a position where God could help me. I made the choice to swallow my pride and put my total faith in Jesus Christ. When I put my life in His hands, I was free. Praise God, He set me free!"

THE STORY OF PAUL NEAL

"I went to jail in Orange County, Florida, in 1993. I had spent eighteen years locked up in different institutions for crimes ranging from drug dealing to attempted murder. Although I had been in the Orange County Jail previously, many changes had taken place. One of those changes was a program called 'Genesis.' I signed up for it because other guys said it was easy. The next day I was one of only four selected for it.

"The first man went into the Domestic Violence Dorm, the second to the Alcohol Abuse Dorm, and the third to the Drug Abuse Dorm. I knew that I could have been placed in any one of those dorms, but my name was called out for something called the Life Learning Dorm. I asked the CO what that was all about. 'There must be some mistake,' I said. 'Look,' he told me, 'that's where the computer says you're going, and the computer's always right.' I knew I would go crazy if I had to stay in that dorm.

"I knew I would go crazy if I had to stay in that dorm."

"I remember looking through the glass door and saying to the CO, 'Look at those guys. They're praying.' He turned to me and said, 'Yeah, they do a lot of that kind of thing in there.'

"When I finally entered the dorm, they were just starting their morning Bible study class. The man teaching told us to open our Bibles to 'Big John.' I tried to find that in the index, but needless to say, I couldn't.

"Although I thought someone had put me there by mistake, it was not by mistake. You see, God does not make mistakes. Even when we do not understand the purpose, God always has a plan for our lives—because it was in that Life Learning Dorm, sponsored by Good News, that I accepted Jesus Christ as my Savior. Just as God prepared Moses for the work that he was to do for God, I believe God put me in that dorm to prepare me for the work I am to do for Him.

"When I was released, I started a halfway house ministry and began to volunteer at the jail. God led all the way, and today I'm a full-time Good News chaplain in the system where I came to Christ. I tell the prisoners that their lives can be changed also if *they will only open the door and let God in.* I know. I was there. I was one of them. When I had no one to talk to, God listened, and when I cried, He wiped away my tears. I thank God for the day I was put in the Life Learning Dorm 'by mistake.' The experience changed my life forever."

"When I had no one to talk to, God listened, and when I cried, He wiped away my tears."

THE STORY OF DAN MATSCHE

Dan Matsche had been a professional musician for most of his adult life before coming to saving faith in Jesus Christ in 1974. For years, he and his wife, Shirley, had traveled through-out the country and around the world performing in show groups and nightclub bands. They were—and are—among the best when it comes to playing the bass guitar and singing. After his conversion, Dan became a vibrant witness for Christ, and in 1977 began volunteering in a maximum-security jail in Orlando, Florida, where he had been led to minister to prison-ers. Later, after a prolonged daily exposure to jail life and the opportunity for witnessing, Dan felt God's calling to the chap-laincy, and he began his course work at Luther Rice Bible College for ministry training. He graduated in 1981. Dan was the first Good News Jail & Prison Ministry chaplain brought on board by Harry Greene, shortly after he took over as presi-dent of the ministry in 1983. Dan went on to complete his Master's degree from Luther Rice Seminary in 1988.

The Lord used Dan's insights and ministry skills to pio-neer the Good News Life-Learning Program in 1985, an instructional program that is now being successfully replicat-ed through the country and around the world. The Lord is using this biblically based opportunity for prisoners to rebuild their lives. Because of his loyal service to his Lord and to the ministry, in 1986 Dan was named Good News Chaplain of the Year. In 1992, to complement his full-time chaplaincy duties, Dan became a regional director, overseeing chaplains throughout the states of Florida, Georgia, and Mississippi, and in one of the largest jails in the world, Cook County Jail in Chicago. In 1995 Dan was given oversight of the Good News ministry in the state prison system in Hawaii. The next year he assumed oversight for the Good News ministry in Colorado's prision system and relocated to Colorada Springs, CO.

Fourteen chaplins have been placed in Colorado by December 31, 2000. "The ministry is growing so rapidly that Good News brought on another regional director to assume responsibility for my former Southeast jurisdictions," Dan explains. "This meant that Shirley and I were able to move to Colorado to head up the hiring, training, and overseeing of our Colorado chaplains."

In 1986 Dan was named Good News Chaplain of the Year.

At this writing, Dan is providing leadership to the chaplains in the Colorado prison system, as well as to chaplains in California and Hawaii. "The effect of these trained, evangelical chaplains is tremendous as God continues to bring men and women to Christ in greater numbers than ever," Dan says. "The greatest news of all is to see how the Gospel changes ruined lives."

THE STORY OF MORRIS JACKSON

Morris Jackson has had a colorful past. Born in Greenville, Texas, in 1944, he moved to Omaha with his mother in 1965.

At the age of twenty-one, he became interested in boxing and began working out in a local gym. A local trainer soon noticed his raw talent, and it wasn't long before Morris was in his first amateur match—which ended with his opponent lying flat on the canvas, unconscious. From this auspicious start, Morris went on to enjoy a successful amateur career, twice being crowned Midwest Golden Gloves Heavyweight Champion. He turned professional in 1970 and retired with a record of 28-5-1. Some of his career highlights include sparring with heavyweight champion Larry Holmes and knocking out the British heavyweight champion in three rounds in London.

"What a change God made in my life."

However, life would soon become very difficult for Morris. After retiring from the ring, he was arrested for armed robbery, a crime for which he served a sentence in the Nebraska State Penitentiary. Morris was angry and confused, and continued to drift until, through the constant prayers of his wife and mother, he gave his life to Jesus Christ. "What a change God made in my life!" Morris says. "I was soon able to use my God-given gifts not to knock people out, but to uphold them through the power of Jesus Christ."

With a gift for evangelism, Morris has now seen hundreds of men, women, and children come to new life in Christ. He has served as assistant pastor of Freedom Church in Omaha and as the director and teacher of Evangelism Explosion. He also has served full-time as a Good News chaplain since 1992. In September 1997, Chaplain Jackson received a full pardon from the governor of Nebraska.

Morris's duties include overseeing the Life Learning Dorm, a special program in the Douglas County (Nebraska)

Jail, where thirty-six men at a time learn the vital life skills they will need to be productive in society—skills such as how to be a good father and husband, how to handle finances, and how to find and keep a job. In that program, the recidivism rate is approximately 25 percent, compared to 70 percent and above for the general jail population. Morris also has helped establish an Aftercare Program in which newly released inmates are paired with someone in the community who assists the ex-offender in getting and keeping his feet on the ground. In addition, he has initiated efforts to minister to troubled youth in the Douglas County Juvenile Detention Center. As the motto of Good News says, through the power of Christ, Morris hopes *to break the cycle of crime, one life at a time.*

THE STORY OF DANIEL CROCE

"I saw the light in 1985 while serving a two-year sentence at the Plymouth County (Massachusetts) Jail. One day someone gave me a Bible, and I read about a person known as Jesus of Nazareth. I was amazed when I read of the things Jesus both said and did: touching the blind so they could see; ministering to the deaf so they could hear; healing the lame so they could walk. It did not take me long to fall in love with Jesus.

"But, when Jesus started to talk about sin, I suddenly realized I was in trouble. Especially when I read the words, 'But the children of the kingdom shall be cast out into outer darkness: there shall be weeping and gnashing of teeth' (Matthew 8:12). When I saw Christ as He is portrayed in Holy Scripture, I started to see myself for who I really was. When I saw perfection—Jesus—I recognized how far short I had missed the mark.

"On the following Sunday, when the chapel call came, I yelled out my cell number, 16. When church was over, I went up to Chaplain Bob Hanson, and said, 'I'm in big trouble!'

"Bob asked what the matter was.

"I told him, 'I've been reading this Book (the Bible), and I suddenly realized that I've been doing wrong for a long time. All this outer darkness, weeping and gnashing of teeth. Are we talking about hell?'

"Bob answered, 'Yes, Danny, we are. You need to be saved.'

"As the CO motioned with his head for me to move on, Bob said, 'Listen to me! When you get back to your cell, get on your knees and tell God that you know you are a sinner, that you believe Jesus died for your sins, and that God the Father raised Him back up again. Then, ask Jesus to come into your heart.'

"I knew that if I were judged according to my sins, I would surely go to hell."

"I did just what Bob said. In fact, I did it so many times I couldn't count them. I guess I wanted to be sure I was doing it right. I knew that if I were judged according to my sins, I would surely go to hell.

"Overnight, Jesus changed my life. He took away the cigarettes that I had smoked for almost twenty years—after which I had gone to smoking marijuana, free-basing cocaine, drinking, gambling, and swearing. The Lord took away the desire to do all those things, and He replaced them with a desire to love and serve Him.

"When I was released, Bob told me to find a good Bible-believing church and to become involved in its various programs. I did that too. After serving God in various ministries—teaching Sunday school at Boston Children's Hospital, visiting mentally and physically handicapped children and sharing

Christ with them, starting the Christian Basketball Outreach League, and visiting jails and prisons to tell other inmates about the Lord—I began to sense the Lord's calling in my life.

"In September 1991, I started my freshman year at Wheaton College in Illinois. Two years later, as my wife and I were praying about God's leading and guidance for His will in our lives, Chaplain Bob Hanson called us from Massachusetts. He said, 'Danny, they've built a new jail here. It is three times as large as the old facility. The Sheriff wants me to come on full-time and I can't do it. I want you to pray about coming back here after school as the chaplain.' My wife and I prayed about it. Two years later I graduated with a B.A. in Bible and Theology.

"A few nights before graduation, Don Smarto, Director of the Institute for Prison Ministries at Wheaton College, took my wife and me out for dinner. He asked us about our ministry plans for the future. We told him we were praying about going back to the same jail in Massachusetts where I received Christ. Don told us that he was on the Board of Good News Jail & Prison Ministry, a mission that places chaplains in jails and prisons throughout the country and overseas. He then asked us to pray about coming on staff with Good News.

"I love my work, and I love my Lord."

"I was ordained in July 1995 and immediately began the application process to join the ministry. After getting 50 percent of my support committed, I was able to begin as chaplain in the Plymouth County Correctional Facility on October 1, 1996. Chaplain Bob Hanson, who has been ministering here for seventeen years, has helped me, counseled me, and continues to be my mentor and friend in every situation. I love my work, and I love my Lord. The greatest thrill for me is to see lives changed by the power and the Person of Jesus Christ."

* * * *

The preceding testimonies of Good News chaplains are but a brief insight into the people whom God has called to minister to the least, the last, and the lost—in other words, *those people*. Good News chaplains come from many and varied backgrounds and denominations, uniting in Christ in a committed, focused effort to take the Gospel behind bars. These men and women are truly "heroes behind walls," for they have as difficult and challenging a ministry as can be found anywhere.

To find out more about the men and women God has called to be chaplains, we encourage you to visit the Good News Web site at www.goodnewsjail.org. Every chaplain is listed, along with his or her biography, the site of their ministry, and information pertaining to their facility. We also encourage you to listen to our radio program, *Full Pardon*, which can be heard on the Internet site. On this program you will hear true stories of changed lives that have come about as a result of our chaplains' ministry.

The chaplaincy is not glamorous work, but it is a fulfilling and satisfying ministry.

The chaplaincy is not glamorous work. In fact, our chaplains receive little praise for the work they do. However, it is a fulfilling and satisfying ministry, for each day it demonstrates how God can take a person whom society has regarded as worthless and unchangeable and change that person from the inside out, breaking the cycle of crime.

If you want to spend a day seeing someone excited about God's presence in people's lives, just ask former convict Harry Greene about the value of Good News chaplains in the lives of those behind bars. As he shares his heart for the ministry of Good News, he is also realistic about the challenges that face these behind-the-walls ministers of the Gospel. "You must have a sense of humor in this job," Harry says. "You must be willing to be hurt, and you must be willing to be disappointed. You've got to know it's going to happen. You must know that you'll be conned, and you must know that prisoners will take advantage of you. That's a given . . . *and you must know it's probably going to happen 50 percent of the time.*

Today, the diversity of Good News chaplains is the strength of the ministry.

"Our chaplains deal with the reality that working in their mission field *can* result in their becoming emotionally, spiritually, and mentally wrecked. That's because someone they thought was real sincere was actually playing a game with them. That will happen; that's who you're dealing with in prison. But we don't worry so much about the percentage of 'honest responses.' We simply thank God for those lives that *are* changed. We all know of faithful missionaries who minister their hearts out overseas, and in, say, a ten-year period, they may see only three individuals come to Christ. Yes, it's probably discouraging, but we rejoice in the salvation of even a few. We neither question their abilities nor criticize their results. It's the same thing as we minister in jails and prisons. Our job is simply to be faithful witnesses to the faith that is within us."

Today, the diversity of Good News chaplains is the strength of the ministry. As Good News supplies chaplains from New York to Florida, from Virginia to Hawaii—with a growing chaplaincy in Estonia, Latvia, Nigeria, Kenya, Uganda, and India—the ministry feels more blessed than at any time in its history. Harry says, "The international opportunities now before us are staggering in that we are literally being begged for help, much like the urgency of the Macedonian call that went out to the apostle Paul. For that reason, the Good News Board has taken up even greater challenges and has determined that we will respond positively to every request for help—as God enables us to do so.

"For example, as of this writing, it appears that we will have forty or more chaplains placed in India's prisons by the end of 2001. The former Baltic Soviet Union states of Lithuania, Ukraine, and Siberia, and other countries in the region, are also asking us for chaplains. So are nations in Africa, South America, and Central America—even as unprecedented numbers of requests continue to come to us for chaplains in U.S. jails and prisons."

It's been said that God's reward for a job well done is that He promises to give us an even bigger job to do. That's why Harry is so grateful for chaplains who love the Lord, have compassion on our nation's—and world's—prisoners, and live to see lives changed by the power, grace, and majesty of Jesus Christ. "I also know," Harry says, "that the best is yet to come—that's where the *bigger job* comes into play. And that's why Good News has initiated Vision 2000 . . . and Beyond, a plan developed in prayer and fasting that we trust God will use to help Good News reach more prisoners and see more lives changed for eternity.

"The verse at the beginning of this chapter will always be a hallmark for Good News Jail & Prison Ministry—a daily reminder of why God has called us to share the Good News of Jesus Christ and His love to those who live their lives behind bars ... and who, before God, will always be candidates to receive a *full pardon* in His Name."

> Remember them that are in bonds, as bound
> with them; and them which suffer adversity,
> as being yourselves also in the body.

Hebrews 13:3

Vision 2000 ... and Beyond

Good News Jail & Prison Ministry celebrates its fortieth anniversary in 2001. During these years, God has blessed, sustained, and enabled Good News to grow from one chaplain, Dr. William L. Simmer, our founder, to the largest provider of full-time civilian chaplains in the world. That is a statement that Good News makes with sincere humility, while at the same time praising God for the blessings He has showered on the ministry—work that, at the writing of this book, is in nearly 250 facilities around the globe.

Since 1995, the ministry has seen unprecedented growth. I believe this has taken place because of a vision God gave to me in late 1993, and also because of how the Board of Directors of Good News stepped out in faith in late 1994 to adopt what we have called Vision 2000 ... and Beyond.

In late 1993, the Lord laid on my heart the need to increase our number of chaplains—not to try to become "the biggest or the best," but so that we would have more human resources to lead more inmates and correctional staff to a saving relationship with Christ. I felt we had the only answer to breaking the cycle of crime, one life at a time, and we needed to share that answer, the Gospel, in more jail and prisons here at home and abroad.

I shared my vision with the Board of Directors in April 1994. Board Chairman Robert Thompson then appointed a committee to meet in York, Pennsylvania, in July 1994 and asked these individuals to report their findings and recommendations to the Board at a retreat in October of that year.

The committee met for two days and nights in York, and I don't know that I have ever felt God's presence at such a meeting as strongly as I felt it there. At the close of our time together, the committee determined that our report would consist of a two-step goal:

1. Double the number of chaplains by the end of the year 2000. (At that time, there were sixty-four chaplains.)

2. Beyond doubling the number of chaplains, trust God to allow us to grow to two hundred chaplains by the end of 2000.

When you consider that we accept no tax dollars; that we have to be *invited* to place a chaplain in a jail or prison; that we have to find God's man or woman for these critical positions; that it takes approximately $50,000–$60,000 a year for a single ministry (including salary, benefits, materials, etc.); that it takes approximately two to three years for the Christian community where we have placed chaplains to fully support the ministry locally; that an infrastructure of support staff for the new ministries is required, along with the technological needs; and that we were starting without any reserve funding to apply to Vision 2000, necessitating raising a great deal of money, I think you would agree that the task was indeed formidable! Humanly speaking, we knew this was an impossible task; we also knew that, with God, all things are possible.

The committee made its report to the Board at a three-day retreat in October 1994. After much discussion and a time of individual and corporate prayers to seek God's will, the Board unanimously accepted and approved Vision 2000. We believed the promise of Ephesians 3:20, which tells us, "Now unto him that is able to do exceedingly abundantly above all that we ask or think . . . ." Today, we praise a God whose love and power is not limited by human imagination. God has answered every prayer, and He has met our every need as we have seen Vision 2000 become reality.

Let me share some significant events that have occurred between 1995 and the end of 2000:

- The number of chaplains has more than doubled, and the goal of two hundred chaplains is in sight.

- In 1997 the Colorado Department of Corrections requested that Good News place fourteen chaplains in Colorado state prisons. As of October 1, 2000, the initial fourteen chaplains originally requested are in place. Correction officials have asked us to provide at least eight *additional* chaplains.

- In 1998 Good News assumed support and oversight of thirteen chaplains in Latvia.

- In 1999 the *Full Pardon* daily radio program changed from a five-minute to a two-minute format and the number of broadcast outlets increased dramatically. In April 2000 this radio ministry was made available on the Internet through www.oneplace.com. Narrated by myself, *Full Pardon* shows God's power in changing lives through the ministry of chaplains and volunteers.

- Also in 1999, Dr. Harry E. Fletcher joined the staff as Vice President of Ministry after twenty-five years as a senior pastor, Bible college and seminary president, chaplain, and member of the Good News Board of Directors.

- In February 2000, God opened doors in India to place an additional twenty chaplains.

- By April 2000, three more chaplains were in Latvia, and ten Estonian chaplains joined Good News.

- In fall 2000, requests for chaplains were at an all-time high, with our New Ministry Development staff working on more than thirty-five opportunities to place chaplains in the next year.

- In December 2000, the Good News Web site—www.goodnewsjail.org—made its debut.

During this time God not only sustained the ministries existing prior to 1995, but He also met *every* need we had while allowing us the privilege to see 235,503 domestic and international decisions to follow Christ from *those people*. We truly serve an awesome God, to whom we give all the credit for the results we have seen.

Now, as we look at Vision 2000 . . . and Beyond, we do so in anticipation of God's blessing. Based on new ministries coming online, the two hundred chaplain goal we established in 1994 will be eclipsed in 2001. Our New Ministry Development Department is being inundated with requests for Good News chaplains from jails and prisons around the country. In addition, our international ministry is literally exploding; Dr. Harry Fletcher projects more than one hundred international chaplains by the end of 2001.

I especially thank God for our Board of Directors and their determination to be vision- and faith-driven, trusting God to bless and enable as we maintain the stewardship of the ministry. The integrity and ethics of our ministry have been based on God's principles from its founding by my spiritual father, Dr. William Simmer. As a leadership team, we are committed to those principles as solidly today as ever, and will remain so, realizing the great responsibility we have *always to do the right thing.*

The principle on which Vision 2000 was established will continue to guide us in this manner:

Increased visibility =

Greater name recognition =

Increased support =

More chaplains =

More men and women coming to faith in Christ.

When my writing partner, Robert C. Larson, and I first met to begin writing this book, he asked me what I wanted it to accomplish. I said there were three things:

1. Lift up and honor Christ.

2. Tell the Good News of Jesus through my testimony and others.

3. Lead the readers to praise God for what He is doing through Good News chaplains to bring *those people* to Himself.

I trust and pray that we have met those criteria, and that God has blessed your heart as you have read how He used a chaplain's ministry to reach through razor wire, concrete walls, and steel bars to forever change the life of a prisoner named Harry Greene, by granting him a full pardon, and how that full pardon is, and has been, changing lives through the ministry of Good News chaplains for forty years.

May God bless you in all ways.
In service with you,

Harry L. Greene

For more information, contact:

Good News Jail & Prison Ministry
2230 E. Parham Rd.
Richmond, VA 23228

(804) 553-4090

www.goodnewsjail.org